Back to the Basics

A Holistic Approach to Correcting the Stewardship
Crisis in the African American Church

George W. Banks Jr.

Published by Wheatmark™
610 East Delano Street, Suite 104
Tucson, Arizona 85705 U.S.A.
www.wheatmark.com

Publisher's Cataloging-In-Publication Data
(Prepared by The Donohue Group, Inc.)

Banks, George W.
Back to the basics : a holistic approach to correcting the stewardship crisis in the African American church / by George W. Banks, Jr.

p. ; cm.

Includes bibliographical references and index.
ISBN: 978-1-58736-910-0

1. Stewardship, Christian. 2. African American churches. I. Title.

BV652.1 .B36 2007
253   2007932033

This book is dedicated
to my beloved wife, Claudia Shepard Banks,
my partner in marriage for life and my greatest encourager.
This book is also dedicated to my family:
parents, George W. and Mabel C. Banks (deceased);
sister, Vercie L. Jefferson; brother, Rickey Charles Banks;
son, Rodrick Keith Banks;
and all of "Papa's" kids, Brandon, Briona, JeCori,
Morgan, Nia, Shakira, Susaun, and JeToi (deceased).

Contents

Acknowledgments

I am grateful to the many people who have helped make this book possible. The following is a list of a few of those whom I feel should be acknowledged with special thanks.

This book could not have been completed without the behind-the-scenes assistance of Joyce Harrell, my sister in the Lord; Roberta Robinson; and Kay Moorhead, the world's greatest researcher and personal editor. A special thanks goes out to these godly ladies.

My deepest appreciation, as always, goes to my family. My wife, Claudia, has been unwavering in her support of my calling and the hours spent getting this publication to print. She has prayed tirelessly for me, encouraged me, and believed in me. Her unvarying support was a primary source of motivation to persevere in writing this book.

A special thanks also goes to my staff and the entire Graceland Community Baptist Church family of Santa Ana, California, who over the years processed the timeless and timely holistic stewardship principles written in this book. Having done so, their example of unconditional love for ministry and the minister became a model of acceptance for many African American churches across this nation. They embodied the belief that you don't have to become a "mega" church to implement "mega" ministry.

A special word of gratitude is due to Rita Glenn, my administrative assistant of twenty-five years. Her personal dedication and loyalty involving many hours of time and effort beyond the call of duty was a constant source of support.

I also owe special thanks to the following pastors who challenged me over the years to put in print the many stewardship lectures and sermons I shared with their congregations: Dr. J. C. Wade Jr., Dr. Lester Cannon, Rev. Maurice Bates, Dr. L. A. Kessee, Dr. Lovely

Haynes, Dr. K. Edward Copeland, Rev. Samuel Hinkle, Dr. Billy L. Bell, Rev. A. W. Brown, Dr. Robert Charles, Dr. M. Howell, Rev. Leon McDaniel, and Rev. Earnest Randle.

Also, special thanks to my spiritual father in the faith, Dr. Melvin Von Wade Sr., and his congregation at the Mt. Moriah Baptist Church of Los Angeles, California, who gave me the opportunity to facilitate my first stewardship workshop.

Finally, I am indebted to the leadership of WHW Ministries and Faith Evangelical Seminary. A special thanks is due to Dr. Robert A. Williams for writing the foreword to this book, and to Dr. Michael Adams and Dr. H. Wayne House for their genuine love and constant support. God be the glory!

Foreword

Like a skilled physician who has exercised his diagnostic skills to adequately and accurately diagnose a physical malady and then proceeds to write a meticulous prescription for the cure, Dr. George Banks has accomplished a comparable feat in the writing of this book. He has ventured into the forbidden zones of the African American church and has exposed, as well as explored, the weaknesses in stewardship while expounding upon the strengths that need to be developed.

This book covers all facets of the African American church and the personal lives of its church members. It offers a fresh new perspective with practical and purposeful lessons as examples to teach and eradicate the errors without abandoning intellectual integrity. This book also serves as a comprehensive biblical discussion of the role of stewardship in the life of believers. The whole gamut of stewardship is covered with a practical step-by-step plan for persons and churches to follow. This book is also sensible; therefore, in reading it you will not find any "way-out" intellectual concepts, but real formulas that assist Christians in daily stewardship.

It is my prayer that as you read this book your outlook on stewardship will transform into a new and fresh way of managing God's goods.

Robert A. Williams Jr., PhD
Pastor, McCoy Memorial Baptist Church
Los Angeles, California
President of WHW Ministries

Introduction

This book is about a crisis, an ongoing stewardship problem that affects the clergy and congregations in most African American churches. There is a "stewardship syndrome," which is due, in part, to the lack of expository preaching and exegetical teaching using biblical principles in instructing congregants on how to practice good stewardship.

In the New Testament the word "stewardship," from the Greek word *oikonomia*, refers to the management of a household or household affair. It speaks specifically to the management, oversight, and administration of another's property.[1] Therefore, good stewardship in relation to managing God's possessions would incorporate the faithful practice of managing those possessions by the stewards who have been entrusted with the responsibility.

As far as Christianity is concerned, stewardship today involves Christians managing God's work through the local church. God has appointed all Christians to be His stewards on earth. Stewardship is not an option, as Paul points out about his own calling. Being a steward is a necessary part of believing the gospel, even if it involves sacrificing personal rewards (1 Cor. 9:17).[2]

But now, as previously stated, there is a stewardship crisis in most African American churches. This problem exists because the primary ministry of stewardship is usually only centered on the teaching and preaching of financial stewardship. Consequently, in many African American churches, just mentioning the word "stewardship" creates

1   Strong, J. (1996). The Exhaustive Concordance of the Bible: (electronic ed.) (G3622). Ontario: Woodside Bible Fellowship.

2   Youngblood, R. F., Bruce, F. F., Harrison, R. K., and Thomas Nelson Publishers (1995). *Nelson's New Illustrated Bible Dictionary*. Rev. ed. of: Nelson's illustrated Bible dictionary, Nashville: T. Nelson.

a threatened defensive reaction. Although, let me say unequivocally, I do not minimize the significance of money matters. The Bible has much to say about money matters, and we should not be afraid to address what the Bible says.

However, the purpose of this book is to examine stewardship holistically as it is viewed in scripture. Throughout this book, the term "holistic stewardship" will refer to the overall aspect of Christian stewardship and its relationship with the believer and the local church. I will point out that any teaching on Christian stewardship that fails to focus on the management of a Christian's witness, work, and wealth as a whole is incomplete. Holistic stewardship is intrinsic and geared toward the edification of the whole body. Every area of Christian work involves some aspect of stewardship. Thus, a holistic understanding of Christian stewardship and the proper attitude toward its function in the local church can correct many of the problems facing African American churches.

This book suggests the need to get back to basic stewardship principles using the holistic approach to structure the teaching methodology of Christian stewardship to be taught in African American churches. It suggests that the holistic approach to stewardship centered on biblical principles can correct the crises and serve as an effective model to enhance the development of good stewards.

This book actually focuses on uncharted territory. My research indicates that there are a host of scholarly works and a vast number of resources available on Christian stewardship. Unfortunately, there are few books written about holistic stewardship, particularly from the perspective of the African American church. Those authors who have done extensive work in Christian stewardship have written from the perspective of financial stewardship.

However, in the past two decades, there has been a more detailed interest in teaching and preaching on holistic stewardship in the African American church. Some possible reasons for the added interest could be marital breakdowns, the constantly shifting economy, downsizing in the workplace, loss of jobs, or inflation. It is a common belief among African American leaders that what affects the home will ultimately have an effect on the local church.

Traditionally, the African American church has been an institution that supported and sustained itself through some form of stewardship practice. Though the practices may not all have been undergirded by biblical principles, the African American church has sustained itself.

Many leaders and churches perceive a need for a new paradigm when it comes to teaching stewardship in the African American church. However, I would argue that the problem is not a need for a new paradigm, but a need to get back to the current paradigm. That paradigm is teaching stewardship from a holistic approach as the biblical pattern dictates.

As previously stated, this is somewhat uncharted territory, and there is not an abundance of research on the subject. Much of the information published about the subject has been published in the past two decades. The following is a list of some of those publications:

George Barna, noted author, research analyst, and director of The Barna Group, coauthored a book with Harry R. Jackson Jr. titled *High Impact African-American Churches*. Chapter 7 of that book is titled "Holistic Stewardship." It is very resourceful and offers fairly comprehensive information on the subject. The book examines megachurches and the impact they have on the African American church. It offers concept after concept and proves to be a valuable source of holistic understanding of stewardship.

Melvin Amerson recently wrote *Stewardship in African-American Churches: A New Paradigm*. The book offers practical ideas aimed at helping church leaders lead effectively in the area of stewardship. Amerson is a consultant for the Texas Methodist Foundation. His book offers valuable information, particularly in setting up a year-round calendar for strategically teaching stewardship as a lifestyle from a black perspective.

Lee Jenkins's *Taking Care of Business: Establishing a Financial Legacy for the African-American Family* provides a wealth of material for establishing a financial basis for financial freedom. His book reaches down to the grass roots of the average African American's problem and plight in dealing with finances.

C. Eric Lincoln and Lawrence H. Mamiya coauthored *The Black Church in the African American Experience*, which has proved to be an invaluable source in providing historical data about African American churches and clergy and showing contrasts in clergy compensation.

Dr. Clifford A. Jones Sr., editor of *From Proclamation to Practice: A Unique African American Approach to Stewardship*, uses a collection of sermons, teaching outlines, and practices to depict the biblical foundation of Christian stewardship in the African American church. In his book, Dr. Jones assembles a rare heritage of black preachers, each of whom shares a presentation on the preaching and practice of Christian stewardship.

Christian stewardship is a broad subject. Consequently, it is not the objective of this book to examine every facet of the subject. The book will only examine Christian stewardship from a holistic perspective and offer a model that uses the holistic approach for teaching stewardship in African American churches.

Chapter 1

Why a Holistic Approach to Teaching Christian Stewardship?

Each year for the past twenty-five years, I have been asked to facilitate some twenty to twenty-five stewardship workshops in African American churches. At the end of each workshop time is allotted for questions and answers or comments and testimonies. On one occasion, a lady stood and gleefully said, "I hadn't planned to attend this workshop. Stewardship was not something I placed much emphasis on. I figured the workshop was designed to teach people to tithe and give more money. I didn't need anybody telling me how to give or how much I should give. I give pretty regularly and support the church programs, so I figured this wasn't for me. But curiosity brought me out the first night, and as a result, I couldn't stay away. I am so glad I attended. I finally understand what Christian stewardship is all about."

This is the existing attitude among many believers in most African American churches. In my opinion, this attitude is derived from a lack of understanding that Christian stewardship is holistic in nature. The stewardship witnessed in many African American churches indicates that there is an alarming trend among congregations in this area. The stewardship attitude in many congregations is viewed as a choice or chore rather than a commission with privileged benefits. As a result, many of these churches are experiencing a crisis when it comes to the stewardship of believers. By the way, it was in this workshop that I first introduced holistic stewardship.

Again, I suggest that in most African American churches, a stewardship syndrome exists. According to *Merriam–Webster's Collegiate Dictionary, Tenth Edition* the word *syndrome* is defined as "a group of signs and symptoms that occur together and characterize a particular abnormality."[1] This definition coupled with my twenty-five years of experience teaching and conducting stewardship workshops in black churches across America concur; there is a stewardship syndrome clearly identifiable in the activity of most congregations' stewardship.

In many churches, there is a group that shies away from the teachings of stewardship. For some, the mere mention of the word creates a threatening environment. This could be due to a lack of a system of expository preaching and teaching stewardship using a holistic understanding centered on biblical principles. It is likely that the greatest threat facing many African American congregations is the excessive emphasis put on teaching, and oftentimes preaching, the stewardship of money. In many of these churches, the word stewardship is related only to the teaching of money matters and fund-raising. I reiterate that this book is not designed to minimize the importance of money matters. Its purpose is to suggest a holistic methodology designed to examine the total aspect of Christian stewardship as it is viewed in the Bible and to examine that methodology's importance to the life of the believer and the local church.

Ronald E. Vallet, author of *Congregations at the Crossroads: Remembering to Be Households of God,* suggests that the church suffers from amnesia. He states:

> The church's amnesia is particularly evident in the arena of stewardship. Though many church leaders deny it and argue otherwise, stewardship is a critical dimension of congregational life. Denials of and arguments against this statement reflect a radical misunderstanding of the nature of stewardship. Church leaders are mistaken when they assume that stewardship is only a program to fund ministry and mission in the church.[2]

Vallet's argument seems to mimic the feelings of the leadership in many African American churches. Much of what is noted as stew-

---

1   *Merriam–Webster's Collegiate Dictionary, Tenth Edition,* s.v. "syndrome."
2   Ronald E. Vallet, *Congregations at the Crossroads: Remembering to Be Households of God* (Grand Rapids: Wm. B. Eerdmans Publishing Co., 1998), 17.

ardship today is nothing more than a yearly campaign centered on teaching tithes and offerings, developing programs to raise funds for mission, or holding church annual days to supplement church income. Vallet further states:

> The church is mistaken when it assumes that stewardship is a separate program to fund ministry and mission of the church. Such a limited understanding of stewardship reduces it to fund-raising and barely rises above the survival mentality that is the bane of far too many congregations.[3]

The problem is stated succinctly. The church must never place a restraint on the teachings of biblical stewardship. Therefore, I suggest that it is important to understand the true meaning of holistic stewardship and how it extends far beyond the teachings of money matters—fund-raising, tithing, and offerings. Again we make note, the stewardship of money is only one aspect of holistic stewardship. Other aspects of stewardship must never be minimized; such a narrow scope of teaching risks the development of unbalanced stewards. The stewardship of unbalanced stewards usually yields bad works rather than good works.

Thus, teaching holistic stewardship is necessary for the edification of the local church. This must become replete in the minds of church leaders. Every area of Christian work involves the believer's stewardship. For example, a believer's worship is affected by his stewardship. *One cannot rightfully worship God in principle and be a bad steward in practice.* Whether we are addressing the areas of leadership, fellowship, or discipleship, all these "ships" are rooted in stewardship. A believer's conduct is centered on his stewardship. Jesus's demands are uncompromising: "If you love Me, keep My commandments."[4]

The importance of teaching holistic stewardship is also crucial because it addresses stewardship in relation to Christian ministry and its future consequence as it relates to the believer's discipleship. To discuss stewardship and not include discipleship would invariably

3   Ibid., 109.
4   John 14:15 (NKJV).

leave us with no foundation. The reason being, believers are not only disciples of Christ, but stewards over His possessions. Stewardship has to do with possessions and productivity. Discipleship informs believers of their fellowship with Christ and their relationship with one another. A believer's discipleship is tied inextricably with his stewardship. Both call for faithfulness and fruitfulness. Therefore, it is important to have a holistic understanding of Christian steward-ship and the proper attitude toward its function in the local church in relation to ministry.

The New Testament teaches that all believers will appear before the judgment seat of Christ to give an account of their works, whether they are good or bad. This refers not only to believers' discipleship but also to the believers' stewardship. This teaching is emphasized in three places in the New Testament.

1. The first time the stewardship life of the believers is empha-sized in the New Testament is in the book of Romans where the Apostle Paul writes:

> But why do you judge your brother? Or why do you show contempt for your brother? For we shall all stand before the judgment seat of Christ. For it is written: "As I live, says the Lord. Every knee shall bow to Me, and every tongue shall confess to God." So then each of us shall give account of himself to God.[5]

The point is that every believer's works, or stewardship, will be judged. The quality of the believer's works will be tested by fire. Here, Paul draws upon an analogy pertaining to precious metals like gold and silver. They are never consumed when burned with fire. However, wood, hay, and stubble cannot endure fire; they become consumed. Such are the works of believers.

2. The second time that the stewardship life of believers is emphasized is in 1 Corinthians. Paul's words are clear and concise:

---

5   Rom. 14:10–13 (NKJV).

If anyone's work which he has built on it endures, he will receive a reward. If anyone's work is burned, he will suffer loss; but he himself will be saved, yet so as through fire.[6]

In this passage, a careful understanding of the text suggests fire is used figuratively for judgment. Fire does not refer to the eternal fire of damnation but to the evaluation of the believers' works. Fire proves the quality of gold, but it consumes wool, hay, and stubble. As it is evident, the believer's judgment will be broken down into two categories. If one's works remain and are not consumed by fire, he or she will receive rewards. However, if one's works do not remain but are instead consumed by fire, he or she will suffer loss of rewards.[7] It is important to understand this passage. It does not teach the loss of salvation, but it does inform us of the seriousness of serving after salvation.

3.   The third time the believer's stewardship life is emphasized is in the Apostle Paul's second letter to the Corinthian church. Here, he informs us of the coming judgment for believers and the place where it will occur:

For we must all appear before the judgment seat of Christ, that each one may receive the things done in the body, according to what he has done whether good or bad.[8]

These three passages of scripture allude to the gravity of the believer's works and provide a plethora of evidence regarding how essential it is to understand the true essence of Christian stewardship holistically and its eternal ramification. How we spend eternity with Christ will be determined according to how we serve Him on earth. As a result, a greater emphasis on the eternal ramifications of stewardship must become the local church's teaching focus. Therefore, we must never make the mistake of substituting church programs to

6   1 Cor. 3:14–15 (NKJV).
7   *The Nelson Study Bible*, 1917.
8   2 Cor. 5:10 (NKJV).

ease the burden of accountability in developing good stewards for the Master.

Case in point, at many African American churches, church programs take precedence over Christian stewardship. The greatest emphasis is put on strengthening auxiliaries and components that enhance the church program rather than developing good stewards to promote the kingdom of God. But now, Christian stewardship involves the believer's time, treasury, and talents, and the exercise of spiritual gifts in serving Christ and others. This epitomizes good stewardship, which must always take precedence over church programs.

Often the confusion stems from church traditions that place more emphasis on church work rather than the work of the church. The work of the local church is always discipleship, evangelism, and stewardship. Developing church programs is good, but they should never take precedence over equipping saints to become good stewards. Stewards will not be judged according to church programs, but according to their works, whether good or bad, which implies the stewardship of believers. Therefore, I am convinced there is a need to return to the basics and teach holistic stewardship in light of the tenets of scriptures. *A holistic approach centered on biblical principles is a must for teaching believers to become good stewards through the local church.*

Also, in writing this book, I felt the need to address some of the crises many African American pastors face today, particularly in the areas of church structure and organization, church finance, and pastoral care. Getting back to the basics and teaching holistic stewardship can correct these crises.

To begin with, improper church structure and organization has contributed much to the stewardship crisis. As a result, church growth has slowed and many pastors are hindered by those steeped in tradition. For example, too often pastors are held hostage by the old, infamous killer, church bylaws. Many churches are bound and ruled by church bylaws, rather than being bound and ruled by the Word of God.

In my opinion, any church that is solely ruled by bylaws and not the Bible may be just a local church and not the Lord's church. The difference is apparent. *A typical local church belongs to the locals; the Lord's church belongs to the Lord.* To deal with this problem, many pastors seek a new venue and leave a problematic church with its crises. Splitting the church becomes the second alternative.

It is not my intent to discredit church bylaws or to suggest a discontinuation of them. If used properly, these bylaws serve their organizational purpose. Nonetheless, to represent some scriptural resemblance, each article should be undergirded by the Word of God. Scripture declares that the church is a living organism, yet it points out the need for organization. Some form of parliamentary order helps to limit church crises and church conflicts. However, the Bible, not church bylaws, should serve as the rule for church life.

While counseling many pastors who faced severe structural crises in their churches, I was surprised to learn that many had never taught or preached through the Pastoral Epistles (Titus and 1 and 2 Timothy). What great instructions we have from these three letters written by the Apostle Paul to his cohorts in the ministry. When I became pastor of the First Mission Baptist Church of Santa Ana, California (now Graceland Community Baptist Church), the first book of the Bible I taught the church about was the book of Titus. The church was spiritually damaged, structurally damaged, and in need of repair. The Holy Spirit led me to the book of Titus, and each Sunday my introduction began with, "For this reason I left you in Crete, that you should set in order the things that are lacking."[9] It is important to understand that some churches present a difficult challenge to a pastor, but I believe that *God's people, given the facts, will normally do the right thing.* The Pastoral Epistles gives God's people the information they need to make the right decisions. These epistles present a biblical foundation for church structure and organization. It is impossible to build a stewardship church when the church is hindered by structural damages and improper organization.

But now, teaching holistic stewardship can also aid in eliminating the financial burdens that exist in many African American churches. Holistic stewardship seeks out spiritual maturity. One of the most critical areas of spiritual immaturity is financing the work of the ministry; spiritual immaturity is even more prevalent in caring for the minister financially. In many African American churches, a rather large percentage of people struggle with giving. Whether this is due

9   Titus 1:3 (NKJV).

to the congregation's beliefs or disbeliefs, faith or doubt, giving is still a struggle. If the African American church has a weakness, it is in the area of economics and finance.[10]

Because of financial struggles, many church budgets limit pastors' salaries and benefits. Many churches do not provide their pastor with a medical and dental plan. Some do not include a pastor's retirement plan in their budget. As a result, a pastor often finds himself depending on his spouse to work and help provide family benefits. The problem lies in the following possibilities. What if the wife's employment is terminated or illness prohibits her from working? A church should not look to its pastor's wife to help provide family benefits. In another scenario, a pastor may be forced to get a second job to supplement his family's income. In my view, any church that does not financially take care of its pastor is not just in violation of biblical principles but stands in contempt before God.

The Bible is clear and precise; God never calls a pastor, commissions him, and then leaves him confused about how he should be compensated and spiritually supported. The New Testament is satiated with evidence that God instructs the local church of its stewardship obligation to financially support its pastor just as God instructs the pastor of his stewardship responsibility to shepherd the congregation. Compensating a pastor is a spiritual matter, not a secular matter. The truth involving spiritual matters should be derived from biblical principles. Therefore, if the Bible teaches a biblical principle, then that principle ought to become the fundamental teaching for church practice.

I am reminded of this important lesson. Several years ago, I purchased some exercise equipment for the purpose of toning my body. The equipment arrived unassembled. To save time, I attempted to assemble the equipment without first reading the instructions. The picture of the equipment on the outside of the box became my point of reference. After hours of unsuccessfully trying to assemble the equipment, it became evident that I could not do so without reading the instructions. We can learn a valuable lesson from this—when nothing else works, read the instructions.

10　C. Eric Lincoln and Lawrence H. Mamiya, *The Black Church in the American Experience* (Durham and London: Duke University Press), 273.

This lesson also applies to the stewardship crises affecting many African American churches. Bad stewardship results from a failure to read and follow instructions, the Word of God. Too many churches are struggling financially and suffering spiritually, and pastors are laboring under undue stress. In many African American churches, particularly among mainline churches, pastors are concerned and members are unresponsive. There is a stewardship crisis in many of these churches, and that crisis has a severe effect on both the ministry and the minister. The problem is that the clergy and the laity are failing to read the instructions.

I suggest that defining and structuring the teaching methodology of Christian stewardship enhances the development of good stewards. A holistic systematic model is needed. The model must be developed through expository teaching and preaching centered on biblical principles. Getting back to the basics is the key.

Chapter 2

History and Early Stewardship Practices in the African American Church

The objective of this chapter is to give an overall look into the history of the African American church, the stewardship of slaves, and the slaves' contribution to the formation of the African American church. This chapter will also discuss how and why certain traditions were formed in an effort to financially support the early churches and the circumstances surrounding why some of these traditions are still being practiced in the twenty-first century.

Historical Overview

Historically, African American churches have had a strong tradition of stewardship. It is only recently that many of these churches have strayed from their path of faithful stewardship. Melvin Amerson's book, *Stewardship in African-American Churches: A New Paradigm*, states:

> The African-American church has always had a strong history and tradition of Christian stewardship. Its history and early traditions offer incredible examples of faith in the midst of difficult and harsh situations.[1]

Today, many of these examples are embedded in the archives of American black church history.

During the slavery era, Negro slaves faced unimaginable conditions and hardships; however, they maintained an unshakable faith

---

1   Melvin Amerson, *Stewardship in African-American Churches: A New Paradigm* (Nashville, TN: Discipleship Resources 1989), 11.

in God. In the book *This Far by Faith*, authored by Juan Williams and Quinton Dixie, the authors state:

> As slaves, black Americans were stripped away from organized worship. They came to God not through the church but through faith.[2]

Their faith was first initiated by their will to survive. The authors add that absolute faith and its power touched the lives of people like Sojourner Truth.[3] By faith, Sojourner Truth propelled her stewardship to spread the gospel, disregarding her own safety, in the fight to end slavery.

Major J. Jones in his book, *Black Awareness: A Theology of Hope*, argues:

> No other institution growing out of slavery and the confused time of reconstruction has quite equaled the black church. It, and it alone, has stood as a sure bulwark against despair. It has held in common unity more black people than any other institution and it has had more influence in molding the thoughts and life of black people in America than has any other single agency. In its beginning, it was largely a rural institution. Called of God to serve an oppressed, enslaved people, the black church took the religion of the oppressor and made of it a tool for the survival of an oppressed people, and this it achieved under the watchful eye of the oppressor. The mobility created by the slave trade, the destruction of the black family, and the prohibition of the African's language served to destroy the social cohesion of the African slave. But for the black church as an institution, and Christianity as a faith, the black man would have soon despaired. As Dr. Cone puts it: "But few slaves committed suicide. Most refused to accept the white master's definition of black humanity and rebelled with every ounce of humanity in them; the black church became the home base for revolution."[4]

2   Juan Williams and Quinton Dixie, *This Far By Faith* (New York, New York: Blackside, Inc., 2003), 2.

3   Ibid., 3.

4   Major J. Jones, *Black Awareness: A Theology of Hope* (Nashville: Abingdon Press, 1971), 40.

Major Jones succinctly declares that no other institution's stewardship has had as much of an influence in shaping and developing the lives of its people as the African American church.

In the 1700s, when it came time for church meetings, most African Americans held them underground; however, those who chose to hold open meetings were interrupted by hostile white people on a regular basis. African Americans held their church gatherings underground because plantation owners, fearful that the slaves would rise up and rebel, prohibited slaves from gathering in groups. There were also laws that prohibited slaves from forming their own churches.

With history such as this, why would these slaves want to embrace Christianity?

Again, Juan Williams, one of the authors of *This Far by Faith*, gives us further insight. He asks:

> Why did a people bruised by being sold in slavery and placed in a strange culture that degraded their humanity hold so fiercely to faith in God? By any ordinary measure, it is easy to view God as having abandoned these people. In fact, religion had been stripped, along with names and sometimes family, from slaves to render them isolated, weak, and unable to fight against slavery's oppressive harness. African tribal styles of worship as practiced by the Ibo, Yoruba, Fulani, and other ethnic groups were dismissed in this new world as primitive. White Christians looked down on African worship traditions, with its incantations, ancestor worship, and dancing. And when black people came to white Christian churches, there was little Christian grace. Blacks often had to sit in the back, in the balcony, or even outside. In some cases they had to attend separate services. This perversion of Christian fellowship only added to the difficulty of black people embracing Christianity. But somehow it did not stop them from believing that the God of Christianity was their God too; and the problem was not with God, His church, or His word in the Bible. Faith said the problem was white racism.[5]

Albert Raboteau in his book *Canaan Land* informs us of Denmark Vesey's stewardship in leading slaves to freedom:

---

5   Williams, 6, 7.

Religious duty and a sense of moral superiority occasionally led some slaves to act in the master's interest rather than their own. But religious faith also sustained the decisions of slaves to flee or to revolt, convinced that God would protect and assist them. In 1822, a former slave named Denmark Vesey organized a plot to revolt among slaves in the vicinity of Charleston, South Carolina. Vesey reportedly appealed to the Bible to convert recruits to join his cause, and most of the leaders of the planned rebellion were active members of Charleston's African Methodist church, which was disbanded and destroyed by the white city officials after the plot was discovered.[6]

Austin Steward and Benjamin Paul, both black abolitionists, write:

> Over time as slaves were freed and given property by some of their owners, it became easier to establish open churches. The African American church became the focal point in the community. It became a place where African Americans could not only worship publicly, but it became the place where the community could gather to help one another, share, receive education, and receive information on what was happening in the various communities where they lived.[7]

Albert J. Raboteau, a historian specializing in African American history, further adds:

> Black churches helped form self-help organizations such as benevolent societies that were designed to aid widows, to pay for the burial of the poor, and to teach children to read and write. Moral reform societies also served to foster racial pride and community activism. Through these societies black people acted cooperatively to change the conditions in which they lived. Convinced that progress for the race and escape from poverty depended

6   Albert J. Raboteau, *Canaan Land: A Religious History of African Americans* (New York: Oxford University Press, 1999), 57, 58.
7   Austin Steward, Benjamin Paul, *Austin Steward 1794–1860* [journal online] accessed 13 June 2006, available online http://www.docsouth.unc.edu/steward/support1.html.

upon education, temperance (abstaining from the consumption of alcohol), thrift, and responsibility, black ministers emphasized the importance of moral behavior and self-respect.[8]

Historians specializing in the African American church offer much insight as to how the church constantly drew its people together. In the past and even today, the African American church represents a place of stability, comfort, and strength. In the past, blacks used their churches as bases to create schools for black children. They placed religion and God in particular, at the center of life. They believed firmly in prayer, and it was through incidents such as being pulled from their knees during prayer that provided the momentum to form their own churches.[9]

Basically, there were three types of churches: the mixed church with separate seating for blacks, the separate church under white leadership with white preachers, and the church under black leadership. The church under black leadership was not given much encouragement by whites because they feared it would become a source of rebellion and protest, and in many cases it did.[10]

Though the early African American Christians had no definitive idea of holistic stewardship, it can be argued, as history points out, that the concept was definitely ingrained in their spirits and within the confines of their churches.

Early Traditional Practices

As African American churches progressed and grew, the majority of its members derived much of their livelihood from farming, share-cropping, and domestic labor. With limited employment options, money tended to flow slowly into the African American community.[11] Because of limited finances, many of the churches could not support their pastors.

8   Raboteau, 25.

9   Anne H. Pinn and Anthony B. Pinn, *Fortress Introduction to Black Church History* (Minneapolis: Fortress Press, 2002), 32.

10   Major J. Jones, *Black Awareness: A Theology of Hope* (Nashville: Abingdon Press, 1971), 43.

11   Amerson, 12.

Most churches survived financially through a variety of practices, many of which are still being used today. Church members were encouraged to give to the Sunday school offering, benevolent fund, and solace fund. The general offering was designated for the regular expenses of the church—salaries, utilities, Sunday school literature, other supplies, maintenance, and insurance.

Each auxiliary of the church, such as the usher board, mass choir, deacon board, or mission society would be assigned an annual day to raise funds. On such days, other churches would be invited to attend the fund-raiser and provide assistance in one way or another, usually financial. Pastors would attend with their church choirs, ushers, and members. Members of the host church and visitors would be asked to give money during the collection. Also, they would be asked to purchase tickets for dinners, teas, or other rallies. At times, members were also encouraged to make direct contributions as a means of fulfilling their stewardship obligations.

Clifford Jones reminds us of some these traditional practices in his book, *From Proclamation to Practice*, as he quotes from a sermon preached by the Rev. Milton E. Owens Jr. The sermon's title is "Bread, Wine, and the Tithe." Jones quotes Owens as saying:

> "Many modern-day worshippers have come to accept the sale of tickets for church suppers, rallies, raffles, fashion shows, and other established fund-raising efforts as acceptable practices—although tickets, raffles, and rallies are not what Bible believers could term biblical."[12]

Jones goes on to state Owens's argument:

> These fund-raising endeavors have resulted because worshipers have been unable or unwilling to tithe. Some churches would experience a significant growth in their treasuries if their one-dollar-a-week contributors would place seven dollars in the offering plate

12   Clifford A. Jones Sr., *From Proclamation to Practice: A Unique African American Approach to Stewardship* (Valley Forge, PA: Judson Press, 1993), 94, quote from a sermon by Rev. Milton R. E. Owens Jr., *Bread, Wine, and the Tithe.*

each Sunday—one dollar a day for the many blessings bestowed each day.[13]

Throughout my travels conducting stewardship conferences and workshops, I have found that some of these early traditional stewardship practices are still very much alive. For example, pew rallies are still a means of financial support for the local church. Members of the church are encouraged to invite friends and relatives to fill a pew. Those who fill their pews are celebrated and honored with public recognition and prizes.

The sale of barbeque ribs, chicken, and fish dinners continue to be the main event on Friday and Saturday evenings. Proceeds help provide income for many African American churches. Raffles, fashion shows, and other traditional fund-raisers are also common practices, as are harvest day rallies, king and queen rallies, the twelve tribes rally, the twelve gates rally, the fifty states rally, church auxiliary rallies, and choir rallies.

According to Melvin Amerson, *Stewardship in African-American Churches: A New Paradigm,*

> Rallies always had a goal of raising money, but they were also a source of competition and pride among families to raise the most money. Various groups or families came together to raise money for their church. Typically, there was some form of recognition for the group or family who raised the most money for the rally.[14]

An additional method used to bring funds into the churches involved the Benevolent Society. This was a group life insurance plan sponsored by the church through a mail-order insurance company. The church was co-beneficiary with the survivors of the policyholders. The premium payment and benefit receipts were made through the head of the society. Each time a member/policyholder died, the society received fifty dollars, the church received

13   Ibid., 94.
14   Amerson, 13, 14.

two hundred dollars, and the remainder of the benefit went to the survivor.[15]

In 1983, the Bastian Union Church youth group of Parkersburg, Virginia, began singing in nearby churches as part of their witness program. The church's ladies group began making and selling candy eggs during Easter to raise money to furnish a bus for the youth group. Even when the youth group no longer traveled to sing, these ladies continued to sell candy eggs to raise money for the church.[16]

As is easily seen, history informs us that fund-raising via rally days, competition, the sale of chicken and fish dinners, etc., was normal practice for the early African American church's stewardship. Although these fund-raisers were a means of financing the work of the ministry and paying church bills, there were drawbacks. It was, and still is, difficult for African American churches to stop the practice. Many of these methods continue to be a vital part of the church's stewardship program. Enormous numbers of congregants sincerely believe fund-raising is their means of serving the Lord.

Again, Clifford Jones writes:

> Money raising, especially for debt retirement, controlled a large portion of the energy, time, and ingenuity of many congregations. This caused a considerable amount of concern, sardonic humor, and criticism from within the congregation and from the community. Demands increased as congregations purchased buildings, expanded services, encountered maintenance costs, and met financial obligations for the pastor. An elderly woman, reflecting on this new urgency and the constant appeals for money, said, "All the spirit done gone out of the church; money drove it out." But those that were able to give gave freely, or they made up for it in other ways.[17]

15   Ida Rousseau Mukenge. *The Black Church in Urban America: A Case Study in Political Economy* (Lanham, MD: University Press of America, 1983), 153.

16   Guy Bruce, *Bastian Union Church History*, journal online, accessed 13 June 2006, available from http://www.bland.k12.va.us/bland/Rocky/bastianunion.html.

17   Jones, 110.

Since money was usually tight, support for the ministry of the local church took on an appearance different from white churches. Giving often centered on seasonal harvest. Often the minister was paid with food instead of money. Economic challenges made tithing or regular giving a struggle for most families.

Amerson adds that many churches adopted a plan called "the dues system."[18] As a child growing up in Louisiana, I learned first-hand how the dues system worked. It instituted a fairly simply plan. When churches set their budgets, the amount needed to meet budget demands would be divided among the paying members of the church. The amount assessed became dues for each paying church household.

However, many members made up for their limited gifts by giving their time and talents. Churches needing building additions or building repairs often turned to the congregation for help. The men of the church volunteered their time and talents to lay foundations, erect walls, put up roofs, install plumbing, and paint. Women of the church prepared food and refreshments as the men labored. Sharing skills and talent was a means of contributing. Performing the labor was an offering to God in gratitude for the skill and talent God had bestowed upon them. Members of the congregation put their efforts together for the good of the entire church.[19]

Clifford Jones's contribution to the collection of sermons in his book, *From Proclamation to Practice*, offers this summation:

> These early congregations were energetic and loved their churches and reverends. They used what they had and were creative and intentional in giving to the church. Though the word stewardship was not employed, the concept was implemented. Therefore, the tradition of stewardship in the African American Christian church must not be looked upon with disdain, or with eyes of sympathy and paternalism. Accept this tradition that was creative, unique, and an indigenous experience that was valid and quite successful. African American congregations were—some would argue still are—crisis-oriented, needs-motivated, and project-oriented groups. Thus

18   Amerson, 14.
19   Amerson, 12.

each financial drive had a specific goal: buying hymnals, purchasing choir robes, painting the church, buying pews, and so forth.[20]

Without a doubt, the African American church is still the pillar of the community. Historically, it has been one of the few independently owned and operated institutions that have allowed African Americans to claim their independence and self-sufficiency.[21] Today's African American church faces tough challenges. With the changing of demographics and socioeconomic factors, the stewardship nature of the black church has suffered. Some are calling for a new stewardship paradigm to be explored in order for the church to survive.

However, in my assessment, a new stewardship paradigm is not the answer to the crisis. This is not to suggest that the African American church should not be open to a variety of various stewardship models and teaching tools. However, I would argue for using the old paradigm, the paradigm currently in place, and employing the biblical blueprint that scripture outlines as the foundation for holistic stewardship. Getting back to teaching basic biblical principles and practices from a holistic approach is the key to correcting any stewardship crisis. It is my contention that any problem the Bible does not address is not worth addressing.

Therefore, I believe the first step in understanding holistic stewardship is to begin where God begins with man, and reacquaint ourselves with the stewardship concept in the Old Testament.

20 Jones, 113.
21 Amerson, 15, 16.

Chapter 3

Stewardship in the Old Testament

The present-day church culture generally preaches and teaches the concept of stewardship based upon New Testament scripture. This approach is both logical and sensible because the theology we practice must first be based upon the teachings of Jesus Christ. These teachings are primarily derived from the study of the New Testament. The apostles' inspired and practical instructions, as gleaned from the gospels and the epistles, are as relevant to the contemporary church as they were to the early church. However, to fully understand the holistic concept of stewardship and how it relates to the edification of the body, we must, as author Robert Heerspink states, "Begin where God Himself begins,"[1] and "acknowledge that stewardship originates and is grounded in the Old Testament."[2]

Stewardship in Relation to Creation

The Bible unequivocally establishes God as the Creator of all things and the One who delegates stewardship. One scholar has suggested that in creation, God creates something other than himself; He upholds it, but is not present in it.[3] In Genesis, after the Lord had spoken the natural world into existence, He created Adam and entrusted him with complete dominion over all the earth.[4] The Hebrew word for having dominion is *radah*, which conveys the idea

---

1   Robert C. Heerspink, *Becoming A Firstfruits Congregation* (Grand Rapids: CRC Publications, 1996), 20.

2   Alfred Martin, *Biblical Stewardship* (Iowa: ECS Ministries, 2005), 11.

3   Loren Wilkinson, *Earthkeeping, Christian Stewardship of Natural Resources* (William B. Eerdmans Publishing Company, 1980), 206.

4   Gen. 1:26–27 (NKJV).

of giving care, nurturing, and ruling with benevolence.[5] Further, God blessed the man and woman. He created and mandated that they be productive. Genesis 1:28 reads, "Be fruitful and multiply; fill the earth and subdue it; have dominion over the fish of the sea, over the birds of the air, and over every living thing that moves on the earth."[6]

God ordained Adam, the first human being, as steward over His creation. Genesis 2:15 states that the Lord God took the man and put him in the Garden of Eden to tend, guard, and keep it.[7] Further, the Lord delegated to Adam the responsibility of naming every living creature that he was given to oversee. Only God could create the garden, thus maintaining ownership, but Adam was charged with tending it.[8] Subsequently, all of humanity has been given a dominant relationship over creation. Even Adam's sin and ultimate fall did not preclude him from his role as steward. Adam's willful disobedience did, however, perpetually complicate his ability, and ours, to subdue the earth and her resources as the Lord originally intended. Adam's fall also sealed mankind's fate as temporal stewards over the earth because the breach in man's fellowship with God meant death in the physical sense for every human thereafter. The Lord God makes this clear when He declares to Adam:

> "Cursed is the ground for your sake; In toil you shall eat of it all the days of your life. Both thorns and thistles it shall bring forth for you, and you shall eat the herb of the field. In the sweat of your face you shall eat bread till you return to the ground"[9]

The weeds, plants which attempt to choke out the good vegetation and take over, were not a part of the created order but a consequence of man's sin.[10] Despite man's self-imposed curse, human-

---

5   Ronald E. Vallet, *The Steward Living in Covenant* (Grand Rapids: William B. Eerdmans Publishing Company, 2001), 29.

6   Gen. 1:28, (NKJV).

7   Gen. 2:15 (NKJV).

8   Ben Gill, *Stewardship: The Biblical Basis for Living* (Arlington: The Summit Publishing Group, 1996), 21.

9   Gen. 3:17–19, (NKJV).

10   Wilkinson, 212.

kind still possesses the authority to dominate the world, but only as stewards, not as exploiters."[11]

Author Ben Gill accurately summarizes the necessity of mankind's need to understand this truth by contending that:

> Humans are to oversee the planet for its creating Lord. It is only in the understanding of human dominion as stewardship that a hedge is built to protect creation from the perverted power of humans. When life is not understood as stewardship, then humans use other humans as things and treat the environment as a thing to be exploited rather than a trust to be kept. The human thrust to domination is an awesome divine gift. Kept under the original stewardship command of God, it is the very image of God.[12]

Stewardship in light of man's dominion over creation must also be understood in terms of the covenant relationship God instituted with His people. It is interesting to note that the first usage of the word covenant in scripture is found in Genesis 6:18 where God establishes a covenant to preserve Noah, his family, and a male and female of every type of living creature before He destroys the earth and all its other inhabitants. God ultimately landed Noah atop Mount Ararat and, in Genesis chapter 9, instituted a covenant with Noah, his descendants, and every living creature. Once again, the Lord God commanded that His remaining creation be fruitful, multiply, and abound on the earth giving mankind an even greater stewardship over all the moving things on the earth as well as the stewardship responsibility in how man relates to man.

While God's first covenant included commands, as did all the covenants to follow, it also assured us of His unconditional promises.[13] He pledged that He would never again send a flood to destroy the earth and He set the rainbow in the sky as a sign and seal of His promise to mankind. We should be reminded of God's sovereignty every time a rainbow appears, and we should realize that humanity is God's representative, a representative that aptly illustrates our relation-

---

11   Gill, 22.
12   Ibid.
13   Vallet, 38.

ship to Him as stewards.[14] In spite of man's evil heart and his history of sin, the Lord continued to entrust Noah and all his descendants with the task of managing His creation. Thus, the holistic nature of stewardship continues to unfold as we view stewardship in the Old Testament patriarchal period.

Stewardship in Relation to Old Testament Patriarchs

Abram/Abraham

Stewardship comprised of personal possessions, our modern cultural understanding of ownership, and stewardship that reflects the idea of national blessing are first introduced in the patriarchal era of the Old Testament beginning with the Abrahamic covenant.[15] From the earliest and ensuing mentions of the word covenant, it is clear that God is always the initiator and the covenant is always connected with a stewardship that God has given. In Genesis 12:1–3, God commands Abram to leave his kindred and his place of residence and go to a land that He will show him.[16] This theocratic covenant, which simply means that it pertains to the rule of God, is unconditional and depends solely upon God's sovereign will although Abram must act according to his faith. There is a reciprocal response required that activates the covenant, and faithfulness is expected on each part.[17] As a matter of fact, faithfulness appeared to be the only expectation from God, as there were no stipulations placed upon Abram. This is unlike the other covenants that were to follow.

Later, in Genesis chapter 15, we see the first act of sacrifice in the covenant relationship that was sanctified by an act of stewardship. In the biblical account, God announced to Abram that his offspring would outnumber the stars in heaven and promised the land of Canaan to him as his inheritance. The Lord God then assured Abram of the promise and ratified the covenant by receiving from Abram living sacrifices of a heifer, a goat, a ram, a turtle dove, and

---

14   Ibid., 42.m

15   Gill, 26.

16   Gen. 12:1–2 (NKJV).

17   Iris V. Cully and Kendig Brubaker Cully, *Harper's Encyclopedia of Religious Education*, (San Francisco: Harper & Row Publishers, Inc., 1990), 166.

a pigeon. Yahweh instructed Abram to cut the animals in two, with the exception of the birds, and place them opposite each other. A deep sleep descended upon Abram and during this time a smoking oven and a burning torch passed between the pieces, thus symbolizing God's movement to sanctify the covenant. With regard to the covenant act between God and Abram, Ben Gill writes,

> In the prototypical covenant, the appropriate response to God's covenant with humankind is the offering of a sacrifice, an acknowledgment of stewardship. This stewardship became the actual religious ceremony that sealed the covenant and constituted it as sacred.[18]

The covenant with Abram is renewed more specifically in Genesis chapter 17 when God changes Abram's identity by renaming him Abraham. His new name meant "father of many nations."[19] In securing His benevolent relationship with Abraham, and eventually the children of Israel, God emphasized the other aspects of Abraham's promised stewardship. They included personal blessings, great honor, and a great reputation. In addition, Abraham would later be considered the human source of blessings through his role as the patriarch of Judaism.

Deeply entrenched in the Old Testament Hebrew culture was the notion of inheritance. Custom and law dictated that the son who inherited the father's land was the rightful possessor of that land, hence stewardship beyond the Abrahamic covenant was grounded in the land. God's promise to Abraham that his posterity would possess the land was renewed with Isaac, Abraham's son, despite his character deficiencies, and Jacob, Isaac's son. The land was promised in Deuteronomy 6:3,[20] granted in Leviticus 20:24,[21] and sworn to Israel in Joshua 5:6.[22] The Lord blessed the nation as a whole to conquer their enemies and acquire significant land. He also delegated stew-

18   Gill, 27.
19   Gen. 17:1–5 (NKJV).
20   Deut. 6:3 (NKJV).
21   Lev. 20:24 (NKJV).
22   Josh. 5–6 (NKJV).

ardship of the land to tribes, heads of families, and individuals as the book of Joshua illustrates. The Lord continually reminds His chosen people that they are temporary managers who are bound by His edicts because He is the divine owner of the land. Leviticus 25:23 states this explicitly when the Lord declares, "The land shall not be sold permanently for the land is Mine; for you are strangers and sojourners with Me."[23]

Isaac

Inherent in the view of good stewardship is an understanding of the instructions given by the owner and a willing heart on the part of the steward that leads to obedient action. Just as the Lord God relocated Abraham, so it was with Isaac. In Genesis chapter 26, the Lord commanded Isaac not to go down to Egypt to find food during a famine, but to dwell in the land that He would show him. Isaac obeyed and settled in Gerar where the Lord blessed him greatly. Genesis 26:12–14 states:

> Then Isaac sowed in that land and reaped in the same year a hundredfold; and the Lord blessed him. The man began to prosper, and continued prospering until he became very prosperous; for he had possessions of flocks and possessions of herds and a great number of servants.[24]

God is faithful and unfailing in His covenant relationship with His people. The same covenant blessings experienced by Abraham were promised to Isaac and fulfilled. Likewise, Isaac, in his stewardship, did not fail to call upon the name of the Lord God Almighty and reverenced Him by building an altar in Beersheba.

Jacob/Israel

God continues to bind Himself by His word through covenant as seen in the life of Jacob. Within the womb, Isaac and Rebekah's twins struggled. Esau was the firstborn. However the second son arrived gripping his brother's heel; thus he was given the name Jacob,

---

23   Lev. 25:23 (NKJV).
24   Gen. 26:12–14 (NKJV).

meaning supplanter. Jacob's name was accurately reflected in his character; he eventually manipulated Esau into relinquishing his birthright. This deception forced Jacob to run for his life. Nevertheless, Isaac bestowed a departing blessing that linked Jacob to the Abrahamic promise and possession of the land.[25] Jacob's sojourn led him to the place where his grandfather, Abraham, had begun his journey. It was at this place that the Lord appeared to Jacob in a dream, confirming yet again his covenant promise of blessing.

In recognition of his belief that he had encountered God Himself, Jacob named the spot Bethel, which means "house of God." A significant event important to our study of stewardship occurs here. Jacob vows at this point that whatever the Lord blesses him to receive, he will return one-tenth.

Ronald Vallet states, "The pledge to tithe was not made under the law, but was a freely given response to God."[26]

Later, in Genesis chapter 32, Jacob wrestles with an angel until his blessing is pronounced, and another event of major importance takes place. Jacob is renamed Israel by the Lord. In acknowledgment of having been in the presence of God and lived, he names the place Peniel.

Vallet further describes Jacob's eventful ordeal:

Alone in the ford, Jacob was wrestled to the ground at night in a surprise attack by a mysterious man, and struggle continued until dawn approached. Even though the blow had a crippling effect, Jacob did not let go. His opponent, failing to prevail against Jacob, struck him on the hip socket, putting Jacob's hip out of joint. When the assailant said, "Let me go, for the day is breaking," Jacob refused, saying, "I will not let you go, unless you bless me." The man said to him, "What is your name?" and he answered, "Jacob." The man replied, "You shall no longer be called Jacob, but Israel, for you have striven with God and with humans, and have prevailed" (Gen. 32:28). Jacob called the place Peniel, saying "For I have seen God face-to-face, and yet my life is preserved." After

---

25   Vallet, 75.
26   Ibid., 77.

being given a blessing and a new name, Jacob now named Israel, released God."[27]

Throughout the entire story of Jacob, God continues to honor His unconditional covenant of blessing and favor on the lineage of Abraham. Despite Jacob's machinations, he is still entrusted with great material gain and reveals a heart for proper stewardship to his God.

Children of Israel

The Hebrews of the Old Testament understood and believed in Yahweh as the divine owner of the land, and their belief was reflected in the law. Laws were specifically designed so that no one individual or a handful of individuals could monopolize land rights. To prevent land from being transferred to those who were already large landowners, the law of the right of redemption was instituted and further supplemented by the law of the year of jubilee.[28] Strong's enhanced lexicon defines jubilee as fifty.[29] Consequently, according to this law, at the end of a span of fifty years, several things happened that essentially liberated those who had experienced economic difficulties.

John MacArthur, noted author and pastor of Grace Community Church in Sun Valley, California describes the significance of these periods in history as follows:

> The year of jubilee involved a year of release from indebtedness and bondage of all sorts. All prisoners and captives were set free, slaves released, and debtors absolved. All property reverted to original owners. This plan curbed inflation and moderated acquisi-

27   Ibid., 83. (Vallet's commentary: "It is interesting to note that word play, in the form of a triple pun, is used to describe that struggle near the Jabbok. Jacob in Hebrew is *yabbok*, Jabbok; the stream is named Jabbok; and, finally, the Hebrew word for "wrestle" is *abaq*, abak. Further, the Hebrew word for "struggle" is *sara*, which is very similar to the Hebrew word for "Israel.")

28   Holmes Rolston, *Stewardship in the New Testament Church* (Richmond: John Knox Press, 1946), 16.

29   James Strong, *The Exhaustive Concordance of the Bible*. electronic ed., H2572.

tions. It also gave new opportunity to people who had fallen on hard times.[30]

We see it reiterated again that although the weight of steward-ship responsibility varied, every Hebrew was assigned to manage and oversee a portion of God's creation. Thus, he would be held account-able. Even those who may have been poor stewards at one time or another, if fortunate to live long enough to experience the year of jubilee, were given another chance to properly handle the resources God had supplied.

Joseph

Arguably there is no better example of faithful stewardship found in the Old Testament accounts than Abraham's great grandson, Joseph. In accordance with God's covenantal promise to Abraham that his lineage would be blessed, Joseph experienced the unusual opportunity to exercise considerable stewardship even in the midst of living as a slave in Potiphar's house. Genesis 41:37–43 indicates favor and blessing so abundant in Joseph's life that Potiphar appointed him overseer over his house.[31] The Hebrew rendering of the word overseer, *paquad*, contains several different nuances of meaning: to appoint, to assign, to lay upon as a charge, to deposit, commit, to entrust.[32] All the varied meanings suggest Potiphar must have per-ceived Joseph's wisdom, leading Potiphar to instill a high level of trust in his abilities. Joseph was appointed steward of Potiphar's household giving him full authority to function as both caretaker and manager.[33] As a result of Joseph's faithful stewardship, Potiphar's household and his field thrived.

Even false accusations at the hands of Potiphar's wife that led to Joseph's imprisonment failed to prevent him from functioning as an effective steward. The prison superintendent eventually selected him as steward of the prison. In every adverse circumstance, Joseph pre-

---

30   John MacArthur, *The MacArthur Study Bible* (Word Publishing, a division of Thomas Nelson, Inc. 1997), 188.

31   Gen. 41:37–43 (NKJV).

32   Strong, *The Exhaustive Concordance of the Bible*, electronic ed., H6485.

33   Vallet, 102.

vailed under the favor God had bestowed upon him, and ultimately he was elevated to chief steward of the land after he successfully interpreted Pharaoh's dream. Ever faithful as the covenant-keeping God, Joseph became the vehicle through which God would preserve his posterity and save many lives. Joseph recognizes the theological implications of Yahweh as the Great Steward who is both the giver to and sustainer of His creation.[34] Joseph's knowledge of the implications is evident when he reveals his identity to his brothers and attempts to interpret God's movements in his life and the lives of God's chosen people.

In this brief overview of some of the Old Testament patriarchal figures, I have attempted to address each man's significance with respect to the concept of covenant blessing and that blessing's link to stewardship. The various facets of stewardship examined again underscore the assertion that God is holistic in His plan and purpose for creation. Consequently, His people must also comprehend this issue of holistic stewardship within the full context of scriptural teaching. It is with this mindset firmly embraced that we seek to understand something of holistic stewardship as it relates to worship.

Stewardship in Relation to Worship

Sabbath Worship

At the heart of Old Testament stewardship was the act of worship that originated with the Hebrew understanding of and acknowledgement of the Sabbath. The Hebrew word *shabbāth* is derived from the verb meaning "to cease" or "to rest." God designated this time, the seventh day in the Hebrew calendar week, as a day of rest from the labor of the previous six days and a day sanctified or set apart because it is when He rested. The Sabbath not only mirrored God's own rest following His labor, which was a model for mankind's behavior, but it was also ordained as a day to remember Yahweh's role as Creator, and in particular, His covenant with Israel.[35]

---

34   Ibid., 105.

35   Earl D. Radmacher, Ronald Barclay Allen, and H. Wayne House. *Nelson's New Illustrated Bible Commentary*, Num. 28:7–8. Nashville: T. Nelson Publishers, 1999.

Biblical scholars and theologians generally adhere to the rationale that the Sabbath was initially designed for man's benefit. An excerpt from *Easton's Bible Dictionary* asserts the following:

> The Sabbath, originally instituted for man at his creation, is of permanent and universal obligation. The physical necessities of man require a Sabbath of rest. He is so constituted that his bodily welfare needs at least one day in seven for rest from ordinary labour. Experience also proves that the moral and spiritual necessities of men also demand a Sabbath of rest.[36]

Obviously, the Lord God did not rest due to His own need; rather, He modeled what has been called the work/rest rhythm because it is essential to creation as He intended it to be.[37] Therefore, the principle and the practice of proper stewardship of the Sabbath observance are important to all of humanity, not just the Hebrew culture.

Another major rationale for Sabbath observance in the Old Testament period lies in the Mosaic Law as spoken from God and recorded in Exodus 31:16–17:

> "Therefore the children of Israel shall keep the Sabbath, to observe the Sabbath throughout their generations as a perpetual covenant. It is a sign between Me and the children of Israel forever; for in six days the Lord made the heavens and the earth and on the seventh day He rested and was refreshed."[38]

For the children of Israel, Sabbath might appropriately have been called a memorial day held in reverence to ensure that they would remain all the more loyal to Yahweh's covenant commitment.[39]

Deeming it a holy day, the Mosaic Law was specific in its instruction of proper Sabbath observance but became daunting in terms of its application. All work was forbidden. Activity as mundane as

---

36   Easton, M.G. *Easton's Bible Dictionary*. Oak Harbor, WA: Logos Research Systems, Inc., 1996, c1897.

37   Vallet, 25.

38   Ex. 31:16–17, (NKJV).

39   Matitiahu Tsevat, "The Basic Meaning of the Biblical Sabbath," *Zeitschrift für die Alttestamentliche Wissenschaft* 84 (1972), 495.

breaking a branch for fire kindling to something as necessary as walking from one place to the next was forbidden. The Sabbath should have been a day of celebration and a time of fellowship with the Lord. Later, Judaism of the Old Testament, with its harsh observances, changed the Sabbath from a blessing to a burdensome responsibility.[40]

Nevertheless, pious Jews believed they could adhere to such stringent requirements thus satisfying the Lord with their ritualistic stewardship. This mode of thought becomes even more pervasive as we examine the Old Testament system of worship through the giving of sacrificial offerings.

Belief System Regarding Offerings

The Old Testament system of worship emphasizes the holistic view of religious faith and its stewardship.[41] The book of Leviticus expressly focuses on the worship and walk of the nation of Israel, showing them how to commune with and serve a holy God through obedience and sacrifice.

Hebrew worship centered initially in the tabernacle and then the Temple. In the time of the patriarchs, the patriarchs themselves functioned in a priestly manner, but the consecration of Levi and his sons introduced the formal priesthood as an institution ordained by God.[42] The priests were charged with the primary stewardship for carrying out the traditions and rituals of Hebrew religious life, and they essentially led Israel in the stewardship and practices performed around the tabernacle and later the Temple.[43]

The sacrificial system of Israel was the focal point of worship for several reasons. First, it was believed that sacrifices were gifts to God as the supreme deity. It was unheard of to come before the Creator, Yahweh, without an offering of something precious and valuable.[44]

---

40   Walther Eichrodt, *Theology of the Old Testament* (Vol. I. S.C.M. Press, 1961), 133.

41   John Drane, *The New Lion Encyclopedia of the Bible* (Lion Publishing), 1998, p 202.

42   Gill, 37.

43   Ibid.

44   Ibid.

Second, the Old Testament points out that the gifts were a form of communing with God.

Author Ben Gill states:

> When the Hebrew worshiper selected the best animal from his flock, laboriously carried the animal to the altar, and heaved it up as an act of physical surrender to Yahweh, the entire process involved a new depth of communion with God.[45]

The idea of God smelling the sweet aroma of the offering, as referenced in the first chapter of Leviticus, expresses the belief that He has acknowledged the sacrifice, and it pleases Him to accept it.[46] Finally, the system of sacrifice made provisions for the Hebrews to atone for sins and the offering was reflective of the giver's repentant heart and disposition.[47]

Types of Old Testament Sacrificial Offerings

A brief analysis of the offerings that comprised the sacrificial system illustrates the relationship between the system and its stewardship principles.

The burnt offering practice required that an entire animal in perfect condition be sacrificed with the exception of the skin. The worshipper laid their hands on the animal to demonstrate that the animal was a sacrifice for their own sins.[48] The offering was given in proportion to the person's wealth and occurred during all major corporate worship services. The offering was presented twice daily and doubled on the Sabbath. As the animal sacrifice was completely consumed on the altar, it symbolized the worshipper's complete commitment to God.[49]

A grain offering of flour or grain, oil, and spice was presented along with the burnt offering. A memorial portion was burnt on the

45   Gill, 38.

46   Eichrodt, *Theology of the Old Testament*. Vol. I, 144.

47   Ibid., 145.

48   John Drane, *The New Lion Encyclopedia of the Bible* (Lion Publishing 1998), 163.

49   Gill, 39.

temple altar,[50] but the remainder was eaten by the priests in the court of the tabernacle. This freewill offering demonstrated thanksgiving and reverence for God, and it showed that God's gifts come from more than one source.[51]

Of particular importance is the precedent established for the stewardship of support for today's minister. The principle is introduced in the book of Leviticus as the various offerings are described, and it is clear that the priests were supported by the gifts of those to whom they ministered. Even today, when support through tithes and offerings is administered properly and used wisely, it allows the minister who practices good stewardship to effectively serve the people of God.

The peace offering was again predicated upon the wealth of the worshipper. The ritual was similar to that of the burnt offering except that only the fat, which Hebrews considered the best portion, was burnt on the altar.[52] The remaining meat was shared by the worshipper and his family. The offering was meant as an expression of thanks to Yahweh for His divine intervention or deliverance.[53] When Hebrew families shared the meal of the peace offering, it was a joyous event in which worship merged with fellowship and communion with God.

The sin offering was offered when a person had sinned against another individual or against God. The sin defiled the holy place and required cleansing. The blood from the sacrifice was sprinkled to symbolize that the defilement had been removed through the death that had taken place.[54] Again, a portion of the sacrifice was given as food for the priest. When the worshipper observed that the priest was unharmed after eating the offering, he was assured that the Lord had accepted his act of repentance.[55]

50   John Drane, *New Lion Encyclopedia of the Bible* (Lion Publishing, 1998), 163.

51   Gill, 40.

52   Patricia J. Alexander, *The Family Encyclopedia of the Bible* (Chancellor Press, 1978), 141.

53   Gill, 41.

54   John Drane, *New Lion Encyclopedia of the Bible* (Lion Publishing, 1998), 163.

55   Ibid.

Other Old Testament offerings characterize the broad scope of stewardship demonstrating that it involved every aspect of life. The sanctification of the firstborn as recorded in Exodus chapters 3 and 13 and Deuteronomy chapter 15 were in recognition of the understanding that life itself is the gift of God.[56] The drink offering of wine was given with the burnt offering. The fruit of the vine symbolized the blessings of God upon Israel. The wood offering is first mentioned in connection with Nehemiah. Huge offerings given at the temple during this time required a proportionately large amount of wood to consume the sacrifices.[57] The wood sacrifice was a great sacrifice in a land where wood was often scarce. The offering of first fruits represented God's direct intervention in the agricultural affairs of the Hebrew people. They believed the presence or absence of rain was solely dependent upon the benevolence of God. As a result, the first fruits were considered to be holy, and only the choicest selections were offered to God. Such giving characterized the attitude that was prevalent among the Old Testament worshipper:

> The practice of giving the first and the best to God functioned as a cornerstone of Hebrew giving. As an abiding principle, it calls for a stewardship that does not give God life's leftovers but rather the first and the best of one's efforts.[58]

The concept of sacrificial stewardship can be witnessed in the construction of the tabernacle. Perhaps the most overwhelming aspect of this type of giving was the wholehearted willingness of the Hebrew people to give. "Then everyone came whose heart was stirred and everyone whose spirit was willing, and they brought the Lord's offering for the work of the tabernacle of meeting" (Exod. 35:21). The people contributed in such abundance that Moses had to restrain the people from giving further.[59] The spiritual result was the equivalent of the visible presence of the Lord; this con-

56   Gill, 43.
57   Gill, 45.
58   Ibid., 44.
59   Ex. 36:2–7, (NKJV).

firmed His pleasure with the act of stewardship on the part of His people.[60]

At another distinct level of stewardship was the sacrificial offering given for the construction of the Temple under David's reign. David assumed leadership in giving by committing substantial personal gifts of gold, silver, brass, iron, wood, onyx, precious stones, and marble.[61] Other national leaders followed his example and gave sacrificial gifts. Indicative of David's profound comprehension that they were not owners but stewards was David's prayer and praise to God following the giving:

> "Now, therefore, our God, we thank you and praise Your glorious name. But who am I, and who are my people, that we should be able to offer so willingly as this? For all things come from You, and of Your own have we given You…O Lord our God, all this abundance that we have prepared to build You a house for Your holy name is from Your hand, and is all Your own."[62]

In concluding this overview of Old Testament stewardship through the presentation of offerings and the rationale involved, there are several principles at work. First, stewardship stems from one's encounter with God; therefore, it is a sacred act of worship. Second, stewardship is motivated by the spirit of the giver, which must be one of willingness, not coercion, and giving must be done with a joyful heart. Finally, stewardship is exhibited by giving sacrificially. This is a radical commitment for the people of God which yields great blessings. Those spiritual and material blessings that come from the steward's obedience are further revealed as the Old Testament concept of tithing is addressed.

Stewardship in Relation to the Old Testament Principle of Tithing

In the Old Testament era, payment of the tithe was an outgrowth of the recognition of God's ownership of the Hebrews' lives and

---

60 Gill, 47.
61 1 Chr. 29:2–5 (NKJV).
62 1 Chr. 29:13, 14, 16 (NKJV).

their possessions. By giving the tithe, the Hebrew people were giving back a specific portion of that which the Lord had prospered them with and entrusted to them.

Tithing Before the Law

The scriptural account of Abraham and Melchizedek, king of Salem and priest over ancient Jerusalem, is the earliest mention of the tithe. Biblical scholars agree that Melchizedek was a type of Christ, as is later revealed in the book of Hebrews.[63] Abraham acknowledged Melchizedek's office as Priest of the Most High God and gave him a tithe of the spoils received from those he had captured in Sodom and other cities of that region. Abraham gave because of who Melchizedek represented, not because he owed the tithe to Melchizedek or was demanded to pay it. The first reference to the tithe sets the precedent for rendering it simply because God is the owner and has a rightful claim to everything.[64]

The second mention of the tithe in the Old Testament occurs in a story about Jacob. On the first night after Jacob fled his home and the wrath of Esau, Jacob fell into a fitful sleep and began to dream. After awakening from his experience, Jacob realized he had been in the presence of the Lord and began to worship Him. In conjunction with worship, Jacob vowed to tithe to the Lord. Although it may appear on the surface that Jacob's giving was contingent upon what he expected God would do for him, Gill states, "In the context of the revelation and with a careful study of the Hebrew grammar, it is best to understand this as a simple promise of devotion."[65] It can also be argued that Jacob promised to tithe because he had observed the practice of his grandfather. Whatever the motivation, Jacob's reverential fear and awe of the Lord God compelled him to commit one-tenth of all the material blessings that he would eventually receive.

Tithing Under the Law

Tithing under the Mosaic Law served to solidify the obligation of the children of Israel to the Lord. The tithe could be given reli-

63   Martin, 24.
64   Ibid.
65   Gill, 63.

giously because it was measurable and concrete. The steward could be certain of his stewardship commitment being ever mindful of the fact that he is not the owner. Rolston states:

> An ownership which is not acknowledged is soon forgotten. But when men pay regularly, a definite proportion of their income to the support of the work of God's Kingdom, they are constantly reminded of the fact that all that they have comes from God.[66]

Essentially there were three tithes given during the time of the Mosaic Law.

1. The first tithe of the Lord's is found in Leviticus 27:30–32 wherein the Lord instructs Moses on the proper practice of the tithe:

And all the tithe of the land, whether of the seed of the land or of the fruit of the tree, is the Lord's. It is holy to the Lord. If a man wants at all to redeem any of his tithes, he shall add one-fifth to it. And concerning the tithe of the herd or the flock of whatever passes under the rod, the tenth one shall be holy to the Lord.[67]

Thus stated, the tithe was again a testament to the principle that God is the owner of creation and everything in it. Man is merely giving back a small portion of what He has graciously provided.

An expansion of the first tithe occurs in Numbers chapter 18. The Levites received the tithes from the people as their compensation for their service in the tabernacle. In turn, the Levites were required to tithe one-tenth of the money they received to Aaron and his descendants.[68] The foundation is established here for the full-time minister to be supported through the stewardship giving of the people. In addition, the minister is also required to faithfully practice the tithing principle.

2. The second tithe, commonly called the festival tithe, appears

---

66 Rolston, 21.
67 Lev. 27:30–32 (NKJV).
68 Gill, 65.

in Deuteronomy chapters 12 and 14. The festival tithe, a tithe of food, was brought to the tabernacle in Canaan where it was eaten in a celebratory feast. All the households, as well as the priests and Levites, shared in the meal.[69] The abiding principle behind this stewardship is the sense of community and fellowship that is derived from giving. There is also the idea introduced here that worshippers should offer their tithes at the appropriate place and with an attitude of joy. This is a principle that will be reiterated later in scripture.

3. The third tithe is known as the charitable tithe, and it is decidedly different in its scope. Deuteronomy 14:28–30 describes the responsibility of the worshipper to give this tithe at the end of every three-year period. The worshipper was to store this tithe within their own gates. The Levites, the strangers, the fatherless, and the widows could eat until their appetites were satisfied. So then, stewards had an obligation to provide for the less fortunate as well as the ministers of God.[70] Deuteronomy 15:4–5 clearly states that the Lord's perpetual blessings hinge upon the givers' care for the needy.[71]

The Old Testament motifs surrounding stewardship lay the cornerstone for the development of our belief systems. There is a totality in the early Hebrews' approach to stewardship that cannot be denied as we juxtapose these teachings with the New Testament doctrine of stewardship. As we more fully examine the scriptures in light of the New Testament, we will conclude that we can only perform faithful stewardship if we are holistic in our understanding and application.

69   MacArthur, *The MacArthur Study Bible*, 268.
70   Deut. 14:28–30 (NKJV).
71   Deut. 15:4–5 (NKJV).

Chapter 4

Stewardship in the New Testament

As has already been examined, the Old Testament gives concrete evidence that the concept of stewardship did not have its origin in the New Testament. Stewardship began with God and His initial relationship with mankind. George E. Brazell, author of *Dynamic Stewardship Strategies,* writes:

> God gave Adam the world and all that was in it except for one thing—the special tree in the midst of the Garden of Eden. Adam was to manage God's world and oversee what took place in it. But God, by placing off limits the tree of knowledge of good and evil, showed that He was the true owner of all the things He had created. Adam was in reality, God's steward. When Adam disobeyed God's prohibition about that tree, he transgressed the principles of stewardship and was branded a sinner.[1]

Brazell further states that God is the author of stewardship. However, although God originally introduced the principle of stewardship in the Old Testament, that concept carries over into the New Testament.[2]

Stewardship Teachings of Jesus

Jesus Himself symbolizes the embodiment of the Great Steward as He demonstrated in His life, His teachings, and ultimately His

---

1 George E. Brazell, *Dynamic Stewardship Strategies* (Grand Rapids, Baker Book House, 1989), 14, 15.

2 Ibid., 15.

obedience to death on the cross whereby mankind's redemption was secured.

Author R. Scott Rodin states in his book, *Stewards in the Kingdom*, that "Jesus Christ ushered in a new reality called the Kingdom of God and called us into it as God's children."[3] When Jesus proclaims that He and the Father are one, we must conclude that our insight into who God is as Father is exemplified in His son. Therefore, the example of Jesus's life and teachings radically alters our understanding of how we are to "frame our lives according to the rule of His (God's) law."[4]

Imploring His followers to comprehend how the Kingdom of God functions and what is required to access entry into it was the focal point of Jesus's teachings. The hope of attaining an eternal home in the kingdom through Jesus should produce a steward's attitude centered on the appropriate handling of material possessions, time, talents, gifts, the physical body, and the spirit. These things essentially comprise the proper holistic stewardship of one's life.

Jesus employed the use of parables as His primary means of expression[5] when He taught stewardship and its connection to the Kingdom of God. Gill asserts that Jesus's use of parables is the most appropriate method to teach stewardship and its accompanying truths:

> The parables are effective language that calls for decision on the part of the hearer. The parables draw the congregation in, and they are making a judgment on the characters in the parables before they realize it. The parables are best understood in existential terms. They speak of life in the world and the Kingdom in terms that relate with immediacy and timelessness to life.[6]

Throughout the gospels, Jesus addresses various facets of stewardship and their relationship to an individual's spiritual condition

---

3   R. Scott Rodin. *Stewards in the Kingdom: A Theology of Life in All Its Fullness* (Dorwners Grove, Intervarsity Press, 2000), 12.

4   John Calvin. *Institutes of the Christian Religion* (Philadelphia: Westminster Press, 1960), 277.

5   Gill, *Stewardship: The Biblical Basis for Living*, 102.

6   Ibid., 103.

using fiscal and economic concepts. For example, the recognition that investing in the Kingdom of God is more important than jewels and treasures is illustrated in the twin parables of the hidden treasure and the pearl (Matthew 13:44–46).[7]

Incumbent upon those who are disciples of Christ is the stewardship of evangelism, which contains promises of reward and yields fruit that brings eternal joy and the mutual partnership of shared privilege.[8] This is vividly displayed in Jesus's analogy of the field and the harvesters found in John 4:34–38. The significance of evangelical stewardship is evident again in the parable of the lost coin, which demonstrates the joy in the presence of angels when a lost soul repents (Luke 15:8–10).

In Matthew 18:23–25, the narrative of the merciless servant, Jesus deals with the necessity of forgiveness among the children of God within the context of God's incomprehensible capacity to forgive. And finally, the parable of the prodigal son recorded in Luke 15:11–32 presents the story of a son who receives his inheritance and exhibits irresponsible stewardship; yet the lesson central to the parable is one of repentance and forgiveness.

The necessity of recognizing human need and addressing it with urgency and compassion is obvious in the parable of the Good Samaritan and the parable of the six brothers (which is commonly referred to as the parable of Lazarus and the rich man). The point is, proper stewardship demands that those who possess material resources respond to those who are struggling, thus expressing their faith through the relief of those in pain and poverty.[9]

Clearly, Jesus's use of parables intends to convey His explanation of stewardship in life. A close, in-depth examination of every parable reveals that in each one, Jesus directly or indirectly touched upon some aspect of holistic stewardship and challenged His followers to respond as those who know God and live in relationship to Him; He challenged them to respond as responsible stewards.

Another prominent teaching where Jesus discusses man's relationship to the material world is in the Sermon on the Mount. Gill points out that even a cursory reading of the gospels (and this text in particular) reveals in Jesus a freedom from the tyranny of the material.[10] Likewise, Jesus repeatedly warns His followers against the folly of pursuing wealth as the greatest aim in life and becoming distracted with the material. A person's desire should be to elevate the supremacy of God's kingdom as their ultimate goal. Matthew 6:33 states, "But seek first the Kingdom of God and His righteousness, and all these things shall be added to you."[11] Jesus stresses to His followers that placing the kingdom agenda as the highest priority ensures the care and provision of God the Father. Faith is grounded in the belief that God will care and provide for His own; it liberates the believer to practice a life of stewardship, which edifies the kingdom.

Jesus preached and taught extensively on the whole of life (holism) as one of dedication to responsible stewardship as believers. He also practiced the principles that he diligently taught. He revealed no anxiety, obsession, or distractions with the material. He instead focused on the work of ministry and receiving the support of His needs from those to whom He ministered. He stayed at Peter's home in Capernaum. Mary, Martha, and Lazarus opened their home in Bethany to Him on a number of occasions. Certain women whom He had healed, Mary Magdalene, Joanna, the wife of Chuza, Herod's steward, Susanna, and many others provided for Jesus from their substance.[12]

Just as He had given and received, Jesus instructed His apostles in like manner according to the biblical account recorded in Matthew 10:7–10:

> "And as you go, preach, saying, 'The kingdom of heaven is at hand.' Heal the sick, cleanse the lepers, raise the dead, cast out demons. Freely you have received, freely give. Provide neither gold nor silver nor copper in your money belts, nor bag for your journey, nor two tunics, nor sandals, nor staffs; for a worker is worthy of his food."[13]

---

10   Ibid., 123.
11   Matt. 6:33 (NKJV).
12   Luke 8:1–3 (NKJV).
13   Matt. 10:7–10 (NKJV).

Although Jesus gives completely different instructions for later apostolic missions, He sets the precedent here for what we view as one interpretation of pastoral support/love offering. MacArthur concurs:

> The point here was to teach them (the apostles) to trust the Lord to supply their needs through the generosity of the people to whom they ministered, and to teach those who received the blessing of their ministry to support the servants of Christ.[14]

Jesus never minimized the expectations according to Old Testament law; to the contrary, He heightened the beliefs of what had been formerly taught. Regarding the issue of tithing, Jesus acknowledges the tithing concept in Matthew 23:23 when he addresses the scribes and Pharisees about paying their tithes of herbs. His condemnation was not in their observance of the law but in their pious external display, which belied the fact that inwardly, they were full of hypocrisy and neglected the moral principles of justice, mercy, and faith.[15]

The condition of the giver's heart and one's inward motivation was of paramount importance to Jesus when addressing stewardship. He indicates that the quantity of one's offering does not make one a noteworthy giver in the account of the poor widow who gave two mites, which is recorded in Mark 12:41–44. Jesus observed that many affluent people gave enormous amounts to the temple treasury. However, Jesus lauds the poor widow for the greatest sacrificial gift of all—two mites that represented all of her livelihood.[16] True sacrificial stewardship earns the commendation of Jesus.

Though this analysis is of necessity limited, it is clear that much of Jesus's teaching reflected a holistic interpretation of stewardship that pointed to the sovereign reign of God over the thrones of heaven and earth. His apostles eventually came to understand the all-encompassing nature of Christian stewardship and embraced those precepts as discovered in the stewardship practices of the early church.

---

14   MacArthur, *The MacArthur Study Bible*, 1410.
15   Matt. 23:23 (NKJV).
16   Mark 12:41–44 (NKJV).

Stewardship in the Early Church

The early church, born on the Day of Pentecost, quickly grew into a community rooted in apostolic teaching and fellowship. Author F. F. Bruce states that the new believers who comprised this first church rejoiced in the forgiveness of sins and the gift of the spirit.[17] The result of the authoritative teachings of the apostles was a fellowship and stewardship derived from the deep sense of the members' unity in the spirit.

According to Acts 2:42, the early church converts "continued steadfastly in the apostles' doctrine and fellowship, in the breaking of bread, and in prayers."[18] Some scholars have suggested that only two things are mentioned in this verse, teaching and *koinonia*, the latter being defined as a participation or sharing in common of something with someone else.[19] The phrase "the breaking of bread," when paralleled with texts like Acts 2:42, 46 and 20:7, 11 suggests that this sort of breaking of bread was part of an act of worship that involved eating, praying, teaching, and singing in homes as well as observing the Lord's Supper.[20] All of these activities constituted koinonia, which led to fellowship as Witherington contends:

> Fellowship is the result of koinonia, of sharing in common; it is not the koinonia itself. Koinonia is an activity which can result in fellowship of some sort, and it can entail things like sharing not just spiritual activities such as prayer but also physical food or other goods in common.[21]

The product of the believers' oneness in spirit, doctrine, and fellowship was the shared stewardship of their material goods. Acts 2:44 states, Now all who believed were together, and had all things in common, and sold all their possessions and goods, and divided

---

17   F. F. Bruce, *The Book of the Acts* (Grand Rapids: Wm. B. Erdmans Publishing Co., 1988), 73.

18   Acts 2:42 (NKJV).

19   Ben Witherington, III. *The Acts of the Apostles: A Socio-Rhetorical Commentary* (Grand Rapids: William B. Erdmans Publishing Co., 1998), 160.

20   Ibid., 161.

21   Ibid, 161.

them among all, as anyone had need.[22] Bruce asserts that the concept of holding things in common was not new because Jesus and His apostles had shared a common treasury, and the pooling of property was practiced by at least one of the prominent Jewish sects of the day.[23] Perhaps in response to these examples, and certainly under the unction of the Holy Spirit, the believers who held property and other resources began to sell those assets and share the proceeds with other believers according to their individual need. The expectation of Jesus that those born of the spirit would exhibit stewardship above and beyond the lawful requirements, i.e., the Old Testament law, manifested itself in the actions of the early church.

In the fourth chapter of the book of Acts, another dimension of stewardship provides evidence that the believers in the early church clearly understood their position as stewards because their behavior indicated the belief that all they possessed ultimately belonged to God.

> Now the multitude of those who believed were of one heart and one soul; neither did anyone say that any of the things he possessed was his own, but they had all things in common. And with great power the apostles gave witness to the resurrection of the Lord Jesus. And great grace was upon them all. Nor was there anyone among them who lacked; for all who were possessors of lands or houses sold them, and brought the proceeds of the things that were sold, and laid them at the apostles' feet; and they distributed to each as anyone had need.[24]

It is evident that surrendered wills lead to transformed lives that will result in a higher level of Christian stewardship. Holmes Rolston declares:

> In the yielding of themselves to Christ, the Christians make Christ the master of their possessions. They no longer assert that what they have is theirs to do with as they please.... For the time being, at least, poverty was abolished. There was not to be found

22 Acts 2:44 (NKJV).
23 Bruce, *The Book of the Acts*, 74.
24 Acts 4:32–35 NKJV.

among these Christians any man who lacked for the essentials of life.[25]

It is interesting to note that the believers' bringing their gifts to the apostles for proper distribution is reminiscent of the Old Testament stewardship of the Levites as dictated by the law. However, the apostles were free to delegate the details of distributing the freewill offerings to others so that they could devote themselves to kingdom business as indicated in Acts chapter 6.[26]

Here we see the concept of holistic stewardship in a different light in that the apostles expressed no desire to be involved in financial matters or serve meals because it detracted from their top priority—prayer and the ministry of the Word. Consequently, the apostles summoned the multitude of the disciples, who may have numbered over twenty thousand men and women at that point,[27] and gave them the stewardship responsibility of selecting seven men who they could appoint to the business of properly allocating the daily distribution to the Hellenist widows. Again, the church displayed unity of spirit in their affirmative response to the apostles as seen in Acts 6:5, "And the saying pleased the whole multitude."[28]

The spiritual fervor of the early church and its resultant holistic stewardship likely offered proof to the Jerusalem community that great power imbued these early believers. God's great grace was upon the new converts, and the sharing of wealth was but one outstanding expression of the Christian unity and fellowship that was achieved in the early church.

Stewardship Teachings of the Apostle Paul

More than any other individual, the Apostle Paul was responsible for the spread of Christianity throughout the Roman Empire. He began proclaiming the gospel message immediately after his miraculous conversion on his way to Damascus to persecute those of "The Way," an early term used for those of the Christian faith. He

25   Holmes Rolston, *Stewardship in the New Testament Church*, 29.
26   Bruce, *The Book of the Acts*, 101.
27   MacArthur, *The MacArthur Study Bible*, 1644.
28   Acts 6:5 (NKJV).

embarked upon three missionary journeys throughout the Mediterranean world and tirelessly preached the gospel he had previously intended to eradicate.[29]

Paul understood the magnitude of the stewardship that had been entrusted to him by Christ Jesus. He declares to the Corinthians, "Let a man so consider us, as servants of Christ, and stewards of the mysteries of God. Moreover, it is required in stewards that one be found faithful."[30] Paul recognized his responsibility for superintending the Lord's affairs here on earth as they related to preaching salvation and establishing the church. In fulfilling his calling, Paul supervised others, but he was ever mindful that he was submissive and accountable to the Lord.[31]

A major focus of Paul's ministry for seven or eight years was a ministry project commonly referred to by biblical scholars as the "Great Collection."[32] The Great Collection was a monetary gift collected from Gentile churches to benefit the destitute believers in Jerusalem, which was an overpopulated, famine-stricken city at that time.[33] Paul's exhortation reads:

> Now concerning the collection for the saints, as I have given orders to the churches of Galatia, so you must do also. On the first day of the week, let each of you lay something aside, storing up as he may prosper that there be no collection when I come.[34]

Robert Vallet cites an observation from a William R. Nelson article that states that Paul's instruction regarding the collection established two important principles:

1. "A consistent pattern of giving and a management princi-

---

29 Ibid., 1688.

30 I Cor. 4:1–2 (NKJV).

31 Millard J. Berquist. *Studies in First Corinthians* (Nashville: Convention Press, 1960), 31.

32 Ronald E. Vallet, *Congregations at the Crossroads: Remembering to Be Households of God*, 42.

33 MacArthur, *The MacArthur Study Bible*, 1758.

34 I Cor. 16:1–2, (NKJV).

ple of delegation."[35] Regarding the first principle, the collection was to be set aside by each individual or family and
brought the first day, i.e., Sunday when they assembled for
worship. The money was to be given weekly and all gifts were
freewill and proportionate to the giver's ability. This teaching
was a drastic departure from the Old Testament concept of
taxation, focusing instead upon a stewardship response solely
motivated by God's goodness.

2. With reference to the second principle of delegating authority, Paul was willing to deliver the offering if necessary but his
preference was to appoint a delegation to handle distributing
the funds.

While the passages in 1 Corinthians suggest a new pattern for
giving, 2 Corinthians chapters 8 and 9 provide the richest, most
specific model of giving in the New Testament.[36] In chapter 8, Paul
commends the generosity of the churches of Macedonia—a liberal
giving that was motivated by God's grace despite the depth of these
churches' own economic deprivation. John MacArthur points out
three elements of the Macedonians' giving that sum up the concept
of freewill giving:

1. "According to their ability." Giving is proportionate. God sets
no fixed amount or percentage on giving, and He expects His
people to give based on what they have.
2. "Beyond their ability." Giving is sacrificial. God's people are
to give according to what they have, yet it must be in propor-
tions that are sacrificial.
3. "Freely willing." In this case, one literally chooses his own
course of action. Giving is voluntary. God's people are not

35   Vallet, 42, a statement from an article cited from William R. Nelson,
"Reflecting on Paul's 'Great Collection,'" *Journal of Stewardship* 41 (1989);
8–19.

36   Frank E. Gaebelein. *The Expositor's Bible Commentary* (Grand Rapids:
The Zondervan Corporation, 1976), 293.

to give out of compulsion, manipulation, or intimidation. Freewill giving has always been God's plan.[37]

Paul elaborated further upon the proper attitude of the giver as being of the utmost importance. "For if there is first a willing mind, it [the gift] is accepted according to what one has, not according to what one does not have."[38] Later in the same letter, he admonishes the believers with these words:

> So let each one give as he purposes in his heart, not grudgingly or of necessity; for God loves a cheerful giver. And God is able to make all grace abound toward you, that you, always having all sufficiency in all things, may have abundance for every good work.[39]

Again, Paul emphasizes an attitude of giving that comes from the heart voluntarily, not an attitude indicative of sorrow or sadness. The sorrowful mindset reflects an attitude of giving motivated by a sense of drudgery and obligation that displeases the Lord. Contrarily, the Lord loves a giver whose heart is genuinely and fervently thrilled with the joy of giving. Paul assures those who practice this type of stewardship that God's grace, with reference to material needs, will abound lavishly in their lives, and those givers will have the means to meet others' needs.

Paul summarizes his teachings on stewardship by comparing the believer's act of giving with God the Father's act of giving Jesus Christ to the people of the world. "Thanks be to God for His indescribable gift."[40] Because God offered His greatest gift, it becomes possible for all those who have professed faith in a risen Christ to exercise joyful, sacrificial, and bountiful stewardship.

Stewardship Teachings of the Apostle Peter

Few, if any, scholars would argue the prominence of Peter among the apostles. Peter was called to follow Jesus early in His ministry. After

---

37   MacArthur, *The MacArthur Study Bible*, 1775.
38   2 Cor. 8:12 (NKJV).
39   2 Cor. 9:7–8 (NKJV).
40   2 Cor. 9:15 (NKJV).

the coming of the Holy Spirit, Peter was empowered to become the leading preacher beginning on the day of Pentecost.[41] It is critical to understand the doctrine of the Holy Spirit, particularly with respect to Peter's teaching on stewardship. Gill says of the Holy Spirit:

> The Holy Spirit proceeds from both the Father and the Son. The Spirit witnesses to Christ, regenerates believers, empowers them, and distributes gifts for Christian service. It is especially in this latter regard that the doctrine of the Spirit touches upon Christian stewardship.[42]

The Holy Spirit bestows diverse gifts upon believers so that the body of Christ—the church—may be edified. Every member possesses at least one gift, which he or she is bound to exercise in the Lord's service, as noted in 1 Corinthians chapter 12 and Romans chapter 12. Peter addresses this particular aspect of stewardship in his first epistle to the scattered believers experiencing great persecution:

> As each one has received a gift, minister it to one another, as good stewards of the manifold grace of God. If anyone speaks, let him speak as the oracles of God. If anyone ministers, let him do it as with the ability which God supplies, that in all things God may be glorified through Jesus Christ."[43]

In the New Testament, the word for the kind of gift Peter speaks of is charisma; it is derived from the Greek noun *charis,* meaning "grace."[44] One can then interpret that the spiritual gift is freely given and received through the grace of God who gives at His discretion so believers might minister to one another for the benefit of the entire body. Peter further stresses that good stewards of God's variety of gifts and talents realize that they are responsible for the resources God has placed within the body.

41   MacArthur, *The MacArthur Study Bible,* 1936.
42   Gill, 152.
43   I Pet. 4:10–11 (NKJV).
44   James Montgomery Boice. *Foundations of the Christian Faith* (Downers Grove: InterVarsity Press, 1986), 608.

Specific gifts are found listed in the aforementioned passages of Romans 12 and 1 Corinthians and appear to fall within two broader categories—speaking and serving. Whether a person's gift falls into one area or the other, each individual must properly manage his gift in order for God to get His glory. Bringing God glory should be the goal of every Christian steward.

Peter also speaks to the stewardship of church elders, admonishing them with these words:

> Shepherd the flock of God which is among you, serving as overseers, not by compulsion but willingly, not for dishonest gain but eagerly, nor as being lords over those entrusted to you, but being examples to the flock; and when the Chief Shepherd appears, you will receive the crown of glory that does not fade away.[45]

Inherent in the task of shepherding is the responsibility of feeding or teaching the flock; this is the primary objective of a pastor. It is also incumbent upon the shepherd to protect the flock as he serves in the capacity of overseer. Noteworthy here is the fact that one of the greatest dangers to the early church, as well as the contemporary church, was the unsound doctrine deliberately taught by false teachers in order to scatter the flock. Solid, scriptural instruction was the first weapon used to combat erroneous teaching that could weaken and destroy the flock.

The attitude that governs proper stewardship always understands that the flock ultimately belongs to God. He has only temporarily entrusted some of his sheep to a pastor to lead, feed, and protect. Those divinely called to this area of stewardship are first warned to guard against an attitude of one who is laboring under duress or strict obligation. These attitudes can lead to laziness and indifference in leading the Lord's people. Pastors should also resist the temptation to dishonestly profit financially from the ministry. This is not to say that ministers should not profit from the ministry; to the contrary, they are worthy of double honor especially when they are apt to teach well. However, an indicator of one who is greedy for filthy lucre is the preacher/pastor who teaches false-

---

45   I Pet. 5:2–4 (NKJV).

hoods in order to increase monetarily as described in the first
chapter of Titus.

Finally, in this passage Peter warns against the tendency to lead
by manipulation and intimidation.[46] Vallet in his book *Congregations
at the Crossroads: Remembering to Be Households of God* states that the
pastor's role is that of a specialist whose main goal is to bring biblical
insights and theological reflection to bear on the ministries of that
congregation as one who has received specialized training and has
been afforded the time to do so.[47] But now, Vallet also offers a word
of caution to pastors in using the specialized training they've attained,
in relating to the people of God. He states:

> The pastor's special knowledge and abilities are not to be used in
> an authoritative style. It is not a matter of the pastor saying, "This
> is what I have learned and therefore this is the way it is." Rather, it
> is the pastor saying, "God has given me particular gifts and called
> me to be your pastor. God has also given each of you gifts to be
> used in God's mission to the world. Our task together is to deter-
> mine what are the ways that God wants us to use these gifts."[48]

It is clear that spiritual leadership must be demonstrated by
example. The shepherd lives before the flock. Ultimately, the Chief
Shepherd, namely Jesus Christ, will return at the second coming and
evaluate the stewardship of the clergy and believers at the judgment
seat of Christ.[49]

46   MacArthur, *The MacArthur Study Bible*, 1948.

47   Vallet, *Congregations at the Crossroads: Remembering to Be Households of
God*, 188.

48   Ibid., 189.

49   MacArthur, *The MacArthur Study Bible*, 1948.

Chapter 5

The Holistic Approach:
Back to the Basics

Thus far, we have looked retrospectively at the origin of steward-ship in the Old Testament, its continuation throughout the New Testament, the stewardship teachings of Jesus, the early church stewardship, and the stewardship teachings of Paul and Peter. Also, we have explored some historical research pertaining to the earliest existence of the African American church and its early stewardship practices.

The remainder of this book will focus on the stewardship crisis and syndromes that affect African American pastors and their churches. Our focus will now shift to examining the crisis and intro-duce the holistic stewardship approach as a means of getting back to the basic biblical stewardship principles to correct the crisis. An analysis of portions of the crisis will be presented. What will follow will be the introduction of several suggested teaching materials that can be used to correct the problems.

Citing an excerpt from the book *High Impact African American Churches* helps us to gain a good understanding of holistic steward-ship:

> True Stewardship encompasses the supervision of every resource God gives us for kingdom purposes: money, material goods, build-ings, relationships, time, information, spiritual gifts and abilities, ideas and truths. So much emphasis is placed on raising and allocat-ing money that we often overlook the fact that the most important resources are not financial, and that God will hold us account-able for the management of more than just our church and family checkbooks. In other words, most believers and churches focus

on financial stewardship. Scripture exhorts us to practice holistic stewardship.[1]

Many African American churches and their leaders do place a greater emphasis on financial stewardship over holistic stewardship. As a result, many of these churches experience a stewardship crisis because the true identity of biblical stewardship gets lost. The overemphasis on the stewardship of money leads many congregants to shy away from any aspect of stewardship. Consequently, a stewardship syndrome effect occurs. I am convinced that getting back to teaching the basic tenants of biblical stewardship using the holistic approach is the solution to correcting this crisis.

For those who are experiencing financial crisis, I contend that the problem may be more spiritual than financial. Further, I would suggest that if all believers are stewards, then all local churches should become "stewardship churches." This could be the key to the crisis. This assessment is based on often used religious jargon heard among African American churches. Case in point:

> "We are a Bible-believing church." "We are a Bible-fed church." "We are a Bible-led church." "We are a praying church." "We are a loving church." "We are a church where everybody is somebody." "We are a friendly church."[2]

These mottos are good in nature; they are also harmless. Nevertheless, I have never seen a church motto that reads, "We are a stewardship church." Perhaps, if a church does consider itself to be a stewardship church, this is predicated upon its strength as a giving church. If the stewardship crisis or stewardship syndromes in African American churches are to be corrected, then the church must

---

1   George Barna and Harry R. Jackson, Jr. *High Impact African American* (Ventura, Regal Books/Gospel Light, 2004), 150.

2   Commentary: These are church mottos or catchy phrases used to identify a church's achievement or indicate its desired goals. These mottos are often found on the back pages of church bulletins, plastered on the walls in church fellowship halls, hung as banners in church sanctuaries, or heard as chants led by the leadership during the worship experience.

get back to the basics and build stewardship churches from a holistic perspective.

The holistic model we will be examining in this chapter and in following chapters can be modified based on the individual needs of pastors and congregations. However, I would suggest that any modification in reference to a biblical principle or church structure and order should not be based on the size of a church or its geographical location. The issue is never quantity; it is always quality. I contend that the often used adage "What works in one church will not necessarily work in another church" is philosophical, not theological. Paul's words to the Corinthians' church were:

"Now, concerning the collection for the saints, as I have given orders to the churches of Galatia, so you must do also."[3]

This scripture definitely offers theological inference and suggests that the order and biblical principle can work in any church. Nonetheless, modifications may be altered in terms of applications but never at the expense of discarding biblical principles.

Also, the subjects discussed in this chapter and those to follow will not be dealt with in their entirety. The objective is to offer a suggestive holistic biblical structure or model to use in correcting the stewardship crises affecting African American pastors and congregations. Again, as stated, the model will include a brief analysis of some of the issues, selective biblical principles, and precepts to use in correcting the issues. We begin with what I consider the most severe crisis: biblical church structure and order.

Establishing Church Structure and Order

Throughout the many years I spent working with pastors and congregations in conducting stewardship workshops, I have found that many of the stewardship problems in African American churches are the result of improper church structure and organization.

In the typical African American church, the most central figure in terms of structure and organization is the senior pastor. Understanding his role is crucial to the function of any local church. He is the Lord's gift to the local church.[4] His primary responsibility is to equip

3   1 Cor. 16:1 (NKJV).
4   Eph. 4:11.

the saints for the work of ministry, for the edifying of the body of Christ.[5]

A discussion pertaining to African American church leadership in the book *High Impact African American Churches* states this characterization of African American church leadership:

> One of the most startling impressions left on white pastors after visiting black churches is the degree of respect and deference given to the black pastor. In most white congregations, the pastor is appreciated and listened to but is clearly seen as a hired hand responsible for providing vision to the lay leaders and congregants who then make the final decisions and implement plans. In contrast, the senior pastor is clearly "da man" in the typical black church. He is given authority, expected to use it, and counted upon by congregants to take the church where it otherwise would not go.[6]

This assessment is quite accurate. However, it is also true that in many African American churches the image of the senior pastor as "da man" is more likely perceived on Sunday morning than at a Thursday night trustee meeting or a Saturday evening deacon meeting.

As was noted previously, biblical stewardship is holistic in nature. It pertains to the whole life of the Christian experience, including the structure and organization of the local church. In many cases, the existing order in many African American churches evolves around what are typically called "pew pastors" who are "da men." These men can be the chairman of the deacon board, the trustee chairman, or members of either of the two boards. At any rate, these pew pastors consider themselves the authorities within the working organizational structure of the local church. Biblically, this practice is out of order. Acts 20:28 establishes proper order: "Therefore take heed to yourselves and to all the flock, among which the Holy Spirit has made you overseers to shepherd the church of God which he purchased with His own blood."

After conducting many seminars and stewardship workshops in

5   Ibid. (NKJV).
6   Barna and Jackson, 46.

African American churches across the country, I have learned that many of the stewardship crises are the result of improper church structure and organization. Correcting a church stewardship crisis should not begin with excessive teaching and preaching on money matters. On the contrary, we must first revisit the basic biblical teachings on the Lord's designed order for His church.

As pastors, we must carefully consider the Apostle Paul's words to Titus, "For this reason I left you in Crete, which you should set in order the things that are lacking."[7] If there are structural or organizational problems, expository preaching and exegetical teaching can correct them.

It is impossible to develop good stewards in a church that has spiritual structural damages or organizational problems. If a pastor desires to build a stewardship church, it must be understood that the process involves consistent holistic stewardship teaching. The first step toward building is to design the new church's structure and order.

According R. Scott Rodin:

> The church cannot form stewards unless it recaptures this holistic understanding of our call to be stewards in God's Kingdom. Stewards are formed through a process of consistent, learned, biblically based teaching. This teaching must be supported by the modeling of stewardship and through the challenge from personal transformation.[8]

Clarifying the Pastor's Ministry

A lack of understanding the New Testament church structure and organization has contributed much to the stewardship crisis. Many times in the African American church circle, a call to the pastorate is not always a call to pastor the church. Instead of a pastor, some churches seek out the best sounding preacher. That is, as in the African American church circle, whether the preacher can "say it" or not. Some churches look for a Sunday morning orator with

---

7   Titus 1:5 (NKJV).

8   R. Scott Rodin. *Stewards in the Kingdom: A Theology of Life in All Its Fullness* (Downers Grove: InterVarsity Press, 2000), 187.

eloquence of speech and the use of intonation in preaching style rather than seeking the Lord's designed gift (the pastor), whose function is to oversee the local church and to watch over the souls of God's elect, whom He purchased with His own blood.[9] The ability to preach should be considered one of the criteria in the calling of a pastor; however, the cultural intonation of preaching styles should not be the determining factor. The Apostle Paul did issue the charge to Timothy, "Preach the Word."[10] In the same charge, he exhorted him to "teach sound doctrine, and do the work of an evangelist; fulfill your ministry."[11]

As the head of the local church body, the pastor's first and foremost responsibility is to rightly divide the Word of God through accurate preaching and teaching so the saints are equipped to do the work of ministry. The pastor must give an account of his stewardship in terms of his faithfulness in leading and feeding the Lord's people. It is his responsibility to make sure that the root of a stewardship crisis does not lie within the structure and organization of the church he oversees. Though some of the congregants may not see the need for a pastor/teacher, the task of maintaining proper structure and order within the local church ultimately falls to the pastor. Clarifying the pastor's ministry as overseer is essential to the stewardship nature of the local church. The New Testament instructions are clear and consistent with criteria and duties required of those who desire the "the position of a bishop [overseer/elder/pastor/teacher], he desires a good work."[12]

Back to the Basics: Sample Lesson

And He Himself gave some to be apostles, and some prophets, and some evangelists, and some pastors and teachers...
Ephesians 4:11; 1 Corinthians 9:11; 13–14

This material is the result of a question that is being raised among believers today: is there really a need for pastors? What makes this

9   Acts 20:28 (NKJV).
10   2 Tim. 4:1–4 (NKJV).
11   Ibid.
12   1 Tim. 3:1 (NKJV).

question quite interesting is the prevailing attitude and activity of the congregants who make up our local churches in the twenty-first century. There is an attempt to shift God's designed structure and desire for His church—a church He purchased with his own blood (Acts 20:28).

Too many of our churches are divisive in spirit and fragmented in structure as a result of ignorance to God's revelation for His church. Every congregation's desire should be, "We want to please God." God works in the world through His church. Therefore, every member in the body of Christ must accept God's structure and design for His church. It begins with accepting and supporting the Lord's pastor—His gift to the local church.

I believe the Bible instructs the people of God how to support pastors of churches. The areas of that instruction are twofold: spiritual and financial. However, before the people of God can successfully do either, several considerations must be taken into account. Use the following tables to compare biblical concepts with scripture references.

His Worth: Ephesians 4:8; 11

Biblical Concept	Scripture Reference
Members of the local church will never successfully support their pastor spiritually and financially until they acknowledge his authority is divinely given.	Read Eph. 4:11—Christ gives pastors as a spiritual gift to His church. **Note:** Other scriptures indicate that God calls and chooses men to shepherd his chosen or elect. 1. Exodus 3:1-4:1–17 » Moses's authority came from God. 2. Joshua 1:1–9 » Joshua's authority came from God. 3. Jeremiah 1:4–10; 3:15 » Authority was God ordained.

Biblical Concept	Scripture Reference
(Continued)	**Note**: Jeremiah 3:15…"And I will give pastors according to mine own heart…" Scriptural cross-references: 1. Acts 20:28 » Elders (pastors) 2. Ephesians 4:11 » Apostles; prophets; foundational gifts (cf. Eph. 2:19–20; Eph. 4:11) » Evangelists; pastor; teacher; functional gifts for today's church (Eph.4:11)
» Obey those who rule over you, and be submissive. They watch out for your soul as those who must give account. Let them do so with joy and not with grief, for that would be unprofitable for you.	Hebrews 13:17 Read John 10:1–10; 10:14–18
1. The Master's sheep are the same sheep assigned to the pastor. 2. Sheep who hear the voice of the Master do not find it difficult to follow their pastor. 3. The Master's sheep and the pastor's sheep are the same sheep.	Read John 10:25–30 Word of Caution: 1. If one has a problem following their pastor, the question could be asked, "Who is your Master?" 2. If the Master's sheep hear the Master's voice, they will also listen to the pastor given to the sheep by the Master.

His work Ephesians 4:12–16

Biblical Concept	Scripture Reference
To equip the saints to do the work of the ministry	Ephesians 4:12
Grow the saints to maturity	Ephesians 4:13
Faith builder through the teaching of the Word	Ephesians 4:14
Accurately divide the word of truth	Ephesians 4:15
Encourage unanimity in the body of Christ	Ephesians 4:16

Commentary: The pastor's assignment is ordained by the Lord. He is the giver of this spiritual gift (pastor/teacher) to the local church. And He gave some to be apostles, some prophets, some evangelists, and some pastors and teachers, for the equipping of the saints for the work of ministry, for the edifying of the body of Christ. Ephesians 4:11–12.

His wages

Note: You may wonder how understanding a pastor's wages can be significant.

Biblical Concept	Scripture Reference
Just as his worth is ordained in his calling, so is his work ordained in his commission. Likewise, his wages are also ordained in compensating him.	1 Corinthians 9:1-14
	Commentary:
The word "ordained" from the Greek word *diatasso* translates to arrange, appoint, prescribe, give order. Literally, to set in place. This suggests that the command indicating how pastors are to be compensated was determined in the eternal mind of God even	1. It is customary that who you work for pays your wages. The pastor of a church is employed by God (Jeremiah 1:5; 10; 3:15; Ephesians 4:11; Acts 20:28). 2. The pastor's worth, work, and wages are tied inextricably together. "And He gave some…" pastor/teacher. (Eph. 4:11) That makes him worthy because he is a gift from God.

Biblical Concept	Scripture Reference
(Continued) before the foundation of the world.	3. But then his work is to "perfect the saints to do the work of ministry." That makes his work special because he works for God. **Commentary:** Surely, God who called the pastor and commissioned him would not leave him confused about how he will be compensated.
The principle the church is to use is the only biblical principle the Lord has ordained. Contrary to what some believe, compensating a pastor is a spiritual matter, not a secular matter.	1 Corinthians 9:11, 13–14 It is done through tithes and offerings. **Commentary:** Tithes and offerings are the only biblical monetary gifts we continue to offer to God. 1 Corinthians 9:13. The Apostle Paul refers back to when God first established a purpose for continuing the tithing principle under the Mosaic Law (cf. Numbers 18:20–24). The purpose now is twofold: » Support the Lord's work (ministries) » Support the Lord's workers (ministers) (cf. Num. 18:20–24; 31 with 1 Cor. 9:13) 1. According to the Old Testament, all the tithes of Israel went toward physical support for the Levites and the priests.

Biblical Concept	Scripture Reference
(Continued)	2. According to the New Testament, Paul teaches that a portion of the tithes and offerings are to be used as wages for the Lord's pastor. New Testament teaching gives no other principle. The principle points out, it is to done individually (Gal.6:6) by God's people. It is ordained by the Lord (1 Corinthians 9:14). However, the pastor's maintenance is reimbursed through the general church's operating expenses. See Appendix C. for an example of a pastor's maintenance sheet.
There are blessings for those who support God's pastors.	1. Paul taught the Galatians saints the same principle that he taught other churches (Galatians 6:6–10). 2. The Philippians saints were taught that God rewards those who financially support His spiritual leaders. » Fruit in heaven's account. (Phil. 4:17) » When you please God, He rewards you (Phil. 4:18). » Financially support your pastor, and God promises to meet your needs (Phil.4:19).

What's the Application

Scripture says, He that hath an ear let him hear what the Spirit saith unto the churches (Rev. 2:7).

Is there a need for a pastor? Yes.

He is God's gift to the local church.

His worth says, yes. His authority is from God.

His work says, yes. He equips God's people to do the work of ministry.

Conclusion

Do not let Satan mislead you. The Master's sheep and the pastor's sheep are the same sheep. Therefore, if God assigns you a pastor, just as you accepted Jesus as Lord and Savior as God's provision for salvation, likewise you must accept His gift—your pastor. The chosen pastor is God's choice to watch over your soul from earth to glory. Anyone else who is giving leadership over your soul is not of God.

Clarifying the Associate Minister's Ministry

Continuing with the organizational makeup in a typical traditional African American church, the most visible figure next to the senior pastor is the associate minister. In many worship services this person's visibility may cover everything from reading the Sunday scripture to leading the worship experience. This person may also teach a Sunday school class or a Bible class. Often, in the pastor's absence, the associate minister is given the opportunity to preach before the congregation. His work is similar to that of an intern who benefits from on-the-job training. An associate minister working within the confines of a local church can be very valuable to his pastor. Therefore his role in ministry should be defined and clarified by the senior pastor and properly communicated to the congregation.

In many African American churches, those professing a call to the gospel ministry are given few or no guidelines regarding their ministry role in assisting their pastors.

In his book titled *Preacher, Wait Your Turn*, Evangelist Manuel Scott Jr. argues that "most associate ministers are in serious need of guidelines to help them assist their pastor."[13] This scenario is often seen in typical African American churches. Traditionally, the lack of clear guidelines for associate ministers can lead to an overstepping of boundaries in terms of authority. This can create much tension between an overzealous associate minister and his pastor. Oftentimes, when an associate is not called to pastoral ministry, a problem arises because that associate must wait his turn. Scott offers poignant suggestions as to why many associate ministers find it difficult to wait their turn:

> » Some associates have an oversized ego. They are so full of self pride that they actually believe they can do a better job than their pastor (Proverbs 16:18).
> » Some associates have an undersized sense of integrity. Here we define integrity as a preacher's togetherness based on his commitment to be honest, moral, dependable, and loyal (Matthew 26:74, 75; John 4:24).
> » Some associates have an out-and-out distaste for authority. If an associate minister thinks he knows everything, he may not want to listen to anything the pastor has to share (Proverbs 12:15).
> » Some associates are addicted to glory and glamour. They feel the need to be in the limelight (Matthews 5:16; 1 Corinthians 6:20; 2 Corinthians 4:5).
> » Some associates have no concept of the pay-your-dues principle. In other words, many associate ministers do not have the foggiest notion of the cost pastors have paid to lead their people (2 Corinthians 11:23–28).
> » Some associates, because they have listened to disgruntled church members, are foolish enough to believe that their pastor is deliberately trying to hold them back (1 John 4:1).[14]

These situations must be corrected in order to prevent spiritual damage to the church's structure and organization. The associate

13   Manuel Scott Jr. *Preacher, Wait Your Turn: Ten Lectures for (Young) Preachers and Pastors* (Manuel Scott Ministries: Los Angeles, 1995), 1.
14   Ibid., 2–3.

minister should understand that he is to aide and assist the pastor in whatever area of ministry the pastor deems necessary; this is particularly true in instances where the associate is able to exercise his spiritual gifts. The associate minister's instructions always come from the pastor. They never come from the people. His respect for and submission to pastoral authority demonstrates faithful stewardship, which may eventually lead to greater areas of stewardship.

Author R. Scott Rodin suggests the approach to a crisis in stewardship should be "to jettison wholesale the entire approach to stewardship and start over."[15] As I pointed out earlier, scripture teaches holistic stewardship. Every ministry within the local church centers on its stewardship; this includes the associate minister's ministry. If a stewardship crisis has developed in this area, the crisis must be corrected. Getting back to the basics is the solution to the crisis.

Back to the Basics: A Handbook for Associate Ministers

The call to preach begins with a call from God. It is always a work of sovereign grace. No one who is called earns the call, merits it, or deserves it. The call is rendered upon the person called as a grace gift. A call of God is always from something unto something else. It is God's invitation or summons to be or to do something different.

1. There is a call to all believers. Every believer has been called by God out of darkness into His marvelous light (1 Peter 2:9). We have been called to live as disciples of Jesus (Matt. 28:18–20); and, thus, we have been called by God to obey Him and carry out the work that we alone have been created by Him to achieve (Jer. 1:4–10; Eph. 2:10). There is no such thing as unemployment in the Kingdom of God. God has work for everyone he has called.

2. God calls some to be leaders. The call to leadership, to full-time Christian service, or to preaching of the gospel is not something to be taken lightly. Such a call is a God-given privilege and an awesome responsibility. Any person who receives

---

15   Rodin, 188.

the call to leadership should experience an inward witness of this call from the Holy Spirit.

3. In any congregation there will be men who are experiencing, or will experience, a call to preach. However, not all who are called to preach are called to the leadership of a church (the pastorate).

In the churches of the African American experience (particularly among National Baptists), those ministers who have been called to preach, but who have not yet been called to the pastorate are referred to as associates, ministers, local preachers, licensed preachers, or sons of the house. Whatever title is used in the confine of a particular local church, it is important that the associate understands his calling, his role, and his responsibility. The following subtopics and their explanations will spell out the associate's role:

Framing the Call

In the typical African American church, when a man accepts the call of God to preach, it is customary that the pastor and the church witness his call through what is commonly called a trial sermon. If the trial sermon satisfies the pastor that the calling is authentic, a recommendation is made to the church to confer a license upon the called brother to preach the gospel. He becomes an intern under the pastor's tutelage; his training station is the church that conferred the license. However, most young ministers tragically frame the license without framing the call. Therefore, it is important that the associate preacher understand the nature of his call. Understanding the call can be broken down into six steps:

Separated: The call of God sets a man apart from the people. Therefore, to be called means to be separated from the mass.

Serving: The call of God does more than separate. The call of God also claims a man for his service. No man is ever called solely to preach. The mark of the call of God is not the claim to simply preach, but a determined willingness to serve. God separates a man from the mass in order to train him to serve. Serving always accompanies preaching.

Shepherding: The call to preach is further intensified when God calls a man to shepherd his flock. The call of God defers from the above only in degree. The first phase separates the man from the mass, and the second phase lays claims upon that man for servanthood, thus anointing him. The third phase is a specific charge to serve a specific people. The man is now more than simply anointed. He is given the assignment of pastor. This assignment comes from God and is verified through the voice of his people in agreement with God for the pastor's call to shepherd His flock.

Commentary

If the associate preacher has not received a divine appointment to shepherd God's people, i.e., pastor of a church, then take note from Rev. Manual Scott Jr.'s book, *Preacher, Wait Your Turn*. Remember, God has enough work for everyone he calls.

Fallacies Most Common to Associate Ministers

Many times, those who accept their call to preach mistakenly feel they are immediately elevated from the pew to the pulpit. Too often there is an expectation to preach in the Sunday morning worship, to counsel, to lead the worship experience. Often the associate's misplaced zeal causes conflict between associate and pastor.

These are some fallacies to avoid:

1. The call to preach automatically confers authority, standing, or status or makes the associate an officer in the local church.
2. That the call to preach brings with it the gift of leadership. The gift of leadership is not automatically conferred upon those who experience the call to preach.
3. That the call to preach can be fulfilled by inadequate preparation. Every person called to preach should seek with all their heart to be trained and equipped for their calling.

Functions of the Associate Minister

The associate minister, one who has been anointed to preach, but does not yet have an assignment, is to help and assist his pastor. His work is decided and designated by the pastor of the church that conferred upon him the license to preach.

Roles of an Associate Minister

1. Provide strength for his pastor
2. Have a profound sense of respect for his pastor
3. Be in agreement with his pastor
4. Be submissive to his pastor
5. Seek to advance his pastor
6. Follow orders immediately and correctly
7. Be an excellent communicator
8. Execute any plan given by the pastor
9. Pray for and with the pastor
10. Pursue academic studies through a bible institute, college, or seminary training
11. Be ready for his assignment

Brother preachers, if you were like me, more than likely you framed your license. I was very proud to have my license to preach hanging on the wall in my home. Having the license to preach was gratifying and stimulating. However, I must admit that my role and responsibilities did not make sense until I surrendered myself to God, my pastor, and my church which gave me the privilege to exercise my gift in ministry.

These words of Jesus should be a guideline for associate preachers: "faithful over a few things make you ruler over many" (Matt: 25:23).

A Worksheet for Evaluating the Associate Minister's Role at Home

Some of the qualifications for a pastor include that he should be blameless, he should be the husband of one wife, and he should rule his own home well. "For if a man know not how to rule his own house, how shall he take care of the church of God" (1 Tim. 3:2, 4–5).

Even though this particular qualification pertains to those who desire the office of bishop, elder, or pastor/teacher, do not forget that an associate is an intern in training for God's divine appointment. The appointment may be the office of pastor. Therefore, it is important to understand God's design for the home. This worksheet is an informal exercise that can be used to make sure an associate preacher understands God's design for the relationships between husband, wife, and children.

**Home attitude, the wife's role
(Gen. 2:18; 3:16; Eph. 5:22–23; 33b;
Col. 3:18; 1 Cor. 11:3)**

_____
_____
_____
_____
_____
_____
_____
_____

The wife's responsibility (Titus 2:4–5; 1 Pet. 3:1–6)

_____
_____
_____
_____
_____
_____

**The husband's role (Gen. 2:21–24; 3:16b; 1 Cor. 11:3;
Eph. 5:23)**

_____
_____
_____
_____
_____
_____
_____

The husband's responsibilities
(Eph. 5:25–33; Col. 3:19; Titus 2:6–8; 1 Peter 3:7)

_____
_____
_____
_____
_____
_____
_____
_____

Commentary

Here is some advice for associate preachers. In teaching your wives, it would help to deal with intimacy and sexuality in your home (2 Cor. 7:3–5).

Father and child relationship

1. Training and teaching your children (Eph. 6:4; Col. 3:21)

_____
_____
_____
_____
_____
_____
_____

2. Home atmosphere

_____
_____
_____
_____
_____
_____
_____

3.   Devotional time, quiet/study time, fun time and free time

_____

_____

_____

_____

_____

_____

_____

_____

One must remember that it is Satan's desire to corrupt and destroy anything that symbolizes Christ and his church. The marital relationship and life at home are a miniature structure of Christ and his church. Satan does not care if you are a preacher. His desire is to sift you as wheat and destroy your home. Remember the words of James, "Therefore submit to God. Resist the devil, and he will flee from you" (James 4:7).

Worksheet: The Associate Preacher and His Pastor

From my own experience as an associate minister thirty-one years ago, I discovered immediately that it was essential to have a good relationship with my pastor. As a matter of fact, the only distinct relationship an associate preacher ought to have among the preaching fraternity is with the pastor who gives birth to him as a son and has oversight over his ministry. It is a tragic experience for those who fail to recognize this as a divine privilege God gives to a spiritual father/son relationship in the confine of the preaching fraternity.

This worksheet is an informal exercise of what an associate preacher ought to understand concerning his pastor.

1.   Having the right relationship

_____

_____

_____

_____

_____

2. Regarding the right fellowship

_____
_____
_____
_____
_____
_____

3. Responding to leadership

_____
_____
_____
_____
_____
_____

Friend or foe? You decide.

Again, thirty-one years ago, I chose my pastor to be my father in ministry and also my friend.

Clarifying the Deacon's Ministry

Arguably, one of the greatest challenges for many traditional African American churches is establishing and maintaining God's design for His church in the area of the deacon's ministry. Many of the current black church leadership structures have their historical roots in the rural, southern, post-Civil War environment.[16] Most pastors were not full-time ministers because rural communities could not afford to provide for them. George Barna and Harry R. Jackson Jr., authors of *High Impact African-American Churches,* wrote the following:

> Thus, while the hired (part-time) pastor did the preaching and other ceremonial duties, the board of deacons ran the day-to-day affairs of the church. More often than not, the chairman of the deacons became a de facto pastor. The head deacon and the pastor had to forge a healthy working relationship since the unity between

16   Barna and Jackson, 59.

these leaders would determine the stability and potential of their church."[17]

Unfortunately, even today, at the heart of the stewardship crises in many African American churches is the lack of biblical understanding with regard to the deacon's role in ministry. Many deacons believe it is their right and responsibility to control the pastor and assume stewardship over areas that have not been biblically delegated to them. Consequently, power struggles between the pastor of a church and the deacon board ensue. This often results in a poor working relationship or no working relationship at all, and produces a crippled, ineffective church. While it is absolutely true that, of necessity, the deacon historically wielded a great deal of authority in the pastor's absence, the office of deacon never supersedes that of the pastor/teacher.

It is incumbent upon the pastor/teacher to educate his congregation on the role and expectations of the biblical deacon. The word "deacon," from the Greek word *diakonos,* is literally a servant who has met the qualifications stated in 1 Timothy 3:8-10, 12-13.[18] This person performs various tasks in the church as delegated by the shepherd of the flock. For example, John MacArthur has described a deacon's role in *The MacArthur Study Bible* from the perspective of a person who works under the direct supervision of the elders.

Dr. T. DeWitt Smith Jr. made the following suggestion in his book, *New Testament Deacon Ministry in African American Churches*:

> If churches are demanding that their pastors be trained, and many arrange for their continuing education so that their pastors remain on the cutting edge of ministry, then they should require, demand, that the deacons who serve in their churches should be trained by their pastors.[19]

Dr. Smith's assessment is quite accurate. The deacon's role in

17   Ibid.
18   1 Tim. 3:8–13(NKJV).
19   T. DeWitt Smith Jr. *New Testament Deacon Ministry in African American Churches* (Atlanta: Hope Publishing House, 1994), 8.

ministry is highly visible in the biblical structure of the local church (cf. 1Timothy 3:8–13). Too often an untrained deacon or deacons can have a false view of their role, therefore causing structural damage. If this scene is apparent in any church, then getting back to the basics using the holistic approach to train the deacon is of essence.

Back to the Basics: A Handbook for Training Deacons

The deacon's ministry is an ordained office within the local church. He is often referred to as a pastor's helper. A deacon functions as an officer only within this local church where he has been ordained and appointed to serve. He exercises no lordship over any aspect of the local church. The name deacon was taken from the Greek word *diakonos,* which simply means servant. It suggests the idea of a "waiter," one who waits on tables or serves others.

Therefore, brethren, seek out from among you for seven men of good reputation, full of the Holy Spirit and wisdom, whom we may appoint over this business (Acts 6:5).

Qualifications: 1 Timothy 3:8–13

Verse eight states that deacons must be reverent, not double-tongued, not given too much wine, and not greedy for money. Verse nine states that they must hold the mystery of the faith with a pure conscience. Verse ten states that deacons should be tested. After being found blameless, they are allowed to serve as deacons. Verse eleven states that a deacon's wife must be reverent, temperate, faithful in all things, and not slanderous. Verse twelve states that a deacon should be the husband of one wife, and his children and house should be run well. Verse 13 concludes with these words: For those who have served well as deacons obtain for themselves a good standing and great boldness in the faith which is in Christ Jesus.

Deacons need to be front-and-center leaders, both doing and encouraging others in all areas of ministry, worship, Christian training school, missions, outreach, fellowship, and special projects. A deacon's motto could read, "supporting the ministries of this church through prayer, attitude, attendance, and stewardship."

Deacons' Ministry with the Pastor

God's plan for deacons is to share together in ministry with the pastors of local churches. In 1 Timothy Chapter 3, Paul informs Timothy of the qualifications for those who lead the local assemblies (bishops/pastors). In the same chapter he lists the qualifications for those who would serve with pastors of local churches. 1 Timothy 3:8 reads, "Likewise, deacons must be reverent, not double-tongued, not given to much wine, and not greedy for money, holding the mystery." The word "likewise" actually places the same servant responsibility upon the deacon. He is a partner in ministry with his pastor.

Deacons: A Team Ministry

Team ministry demands accountability on a monthly basis. Deacons must be reminded that their ministry is a call to serve. Some experiences from the past might sharpen a deacon's desire to serve in a particular area of work, and past experiences in certain ministries will also increase a desire to serve. Allowing personal choice under the Holy Spirit's guidance will enhance the sense of joy and commitment in ministry. However, every deacon must be accountable in a certain area to serve in ministry. Each deacon may solicit other men of the church to aid them in their various tasks.

Suggested Areas of Ministry for Deacon Teams

Hospital/Homebound Visitation Team	Deacons will check with the church office on a regular basis, obtain a list of hospital or homebound persons, visit these people for prayer, and seek to fulfill their needs.
Stewardship Team	This team aids the pastor in making sure the financial needs of the church are being met.
Lord's Supper Team	This team confirms that the deacons are aware of proper attire to be worn for administering the Lord's Supper. It also checks with the deaconesses to make sure everything is prepared properly for that day or evening.

Suggested Areas of Ministry for Deacon Teams

Prayer Team	This team works alongside pastor and prayer coordinator praying for specific needs. This team of deacons also makes sure that all the deacons are informed of special needs. The team meets with the other deacons on a regular basis for prayer.
Baptism Team	The deacons on the baptism team aid the pastor/associate ministers in preparing for baptism. They also lend a hand to the baptismal candidate.
Counseling Team	This team participates with the evangelism ministry in street witnessing. This team makes sure every deacon understands how to fill forms out properly. These forms include receiving candidates for baptism, church membership, restoration, and so forth.
Special Needs Team	Coordinates any special needs that may arise for food, clothing, etc.
Worship Team	Makes sure every deacon is familiar with devotion hymns, prayer, and offertory period.

Goals and Responsibilities of a Deacon

Teamwork may be a familiar concept, yet it is one that is often overlooked when it comes to tasks in the local church. We are accustomed to seeing teams at work in football, basketball, and countless other sports, and we discuss the various strengths and weaknesses of our favorite teams and their opponents. We observe that often the best team does in fact win.

In making teamwork a priority, sports teams are able to gain strength, momentum and a single-minded purpose that gives them an advantage. Teamwork is also a familiar concept for today's lay-church leaders. Laypeople may not always understand the subtleties of organizational charts and job responsibilities; however, most can comprehend what it means to be a part of a team. When the ministry of the deacons is described in terms of teamwork, it is easier for most to understand.

Ask a person to serve as a deacon and he may easily feel overwhelmed and inadequate. Ask that same person to become a part of a team of deacons and he may immediately sense that he is part of something special. He knows he won't be alone. Being part of a team gives confidence. Team members believe they will be coached by one another. Through teamwork, deacons can serve with effectiveness.

Building a Deacon's Ministry Team

1. **Participation in the team-building process is essential.** In sports, coaches get onto the field among the players during practice. They talk about plays, and they also show how things are done. Team builders participate in team building.

2. **Shared responsibility.** A team works together and shares responsibilities.

3. **Alignment of purpose.** Perhaps the most important aspect of team building concerns the purpose of the team. Teams can only be built when there is singleness of purpose. Everyone's attention must be focused in the same direction. Otherwise, teams break down and simply become collections of individuals.

4. **Effective communication.** Building teams requires communication. Teams must know what they are about, what plans are being worked on, and what problems need solutions.

5. **Future focus.** Teams are built with a focus on the future. What is the future toward which the team is striving? In sports, that future may be to win the next game. In deacon service, that future may be to meet specific needs or to build the church's outreach ministry in the community.

6. **Task oriented.** Team members focus on specific tasks that will enable the team to reach its goals. Each team member should understand what tasks must be done and how to do them.

7. **Creative talents**. Each team member brings certain creative talents to the team. Teams are built when opportunity exists for each person's creativity to flow into the team enterprise.
8. **Rapid response**. Teams learn flexibility and rapidly respond to problems and challenges. In building teams, leaders must respond quickly to challenges.

Being on God's Team Is What Serving Is All About

The following is a sample list of duties a team of deacons can be responsible for:

1. Inspecting church grounds once a week and making sure trash and other debris is picked up.
2. Filling the baptism pool.
3. Being in charge of the gardening.
4. Being in charge of building maintenance.
5. Making sure light bulbs are replaced as needed.
6. Opening and closing the church.
7. Aiding the pastor in whatever he needs.
8. The Lord's Supper and offering rotation.
9. Every fourth Saturday, the deacons come together from 8:00 AM–10:00 AM to clean, focus on new ideas, and follow up on existing ideas. This meeting ends with a fellowship breakfast.

Requirements for Deacons

Attendance

Every deacon is expected to maintain consistent and regular church attendance. He is to be present for Christian training school, Sunday morning service, Sunday evening service, Bible study, discipleship classes, and the men's ministry. He is also expected to attend all deacons meetings. The only exception to any of these would be in the event of occupational requirements, illness, or some form of emergency. Every deacon is expected to inform the pastor or church office of his absence.

Stewardship

The deacon is expected to be a faithful steward over that which the Lord has entrusted to his care. He is to be responsible in the way he handles his business affairs. He is to be responsible in the way he handles his financial resources. He is to give at least the tithe and pastoral support, and he should look for opportunities to give more. He is to be responsible in the way he handles the balance of God's resources.

Ministry

The deacon is expected to be an extension of the pastor's ministry to the congregation.

Training

The deacon will participate in all the required training offered by the church for deacons.

Example

The deacon is to set a good example before the congregation. His personal habits should not bring reproach upon the Lord or His church. He should seek to keep his body clean and pure from anything that would affect his witness. He should have a good relationship with his pastor. He should have a good relationship with members of his family. His wife should be a strong supporter of his life and ministry. He should have a good prayer life. He should be an instrument through which God can bless others when he exercises his duty as the pastor's helper and servant to the church. He should be an example of one whose only objective in all that he does is the glorification of God and the advancement of God's Kingdom.

Doctrinal

The deacon should take hold of the pastor's vision for the church. The deacon is expected to know what the Bible teaches and be willing to follow its teaching. He is to be faithful and should fully cooperate with the pastor and the congregation.

Clarifying the Trustee Ministry

Many churches teach that the only two scriptural officers within the confine structure of the local church are the office of pastor/teacher and that of the office of deacon. The former is a indefinite divine calling of God. The latter is an appointment by ordination to serve in ministry within a particular church membership.

Thus, many suggest that the trustee ministry is not a biblical office within the local church structure because there is no biblical foundation for its existence. Most suggest it was created to satisfy a state government requirement for organizational incorporation of local churches, to serve responsibly in the handling of church properties, or to oversee any trusted matters.

However, it is my opinion that through the years the trustee ministry in a typical African American church has turned from a trustee ministry to a tricky ministry. In some cases, the trustees have been falsely led to believe they not only are appointed to oversee church affairs but also the affairs of the pastor. This functional error has created much stewardship crisis in the average African American church. In many cases, this organizational crisis has occurred because of a lack of training. It is also possible that the organizational crisis has occurred because the need for a trustee ministry hasn't been explained.

Some churches, because of autonomy in nature, have moved from a two-board operation to a one-board operation. That is to say, only the scriptural basis for the office of deacon is taught; and out of this, selections of two to three men (or women in some cases) are selected to serve also as trustees.

The ministry of trustees can function effectively if men, whose stewardship responsibility is to oversee their particular work, are trained by their pastor. However, if conflict exists here, it will create a stewardship crisis. The crisis must be dealt with and corrected.

Some pastors have written their own qualifications and job descriptions for the trustee ministry. This usually appears to work well within the structure. The Trustee Manual from The New Pilgrim Rest Baptist Church of Dallas, Texas, is an excellent guide to consider for trustee training. See Appendix A for a discussion of the trustee's ministry.

Clarifying the Bylaws Issue

As previously stated in the introduction of this book, it is not my intent to discredit church bylaws or suggest a discontinuation. They serve their organizational purpose if used properly. However, again I suggest that each article of the bylaws should be undergirded by the Word of God.

An Example of a Church Bylaw with Scripture References

CONSTITUTION AND BYLAWS
(Date)

ARTICLE I
NAME

The name of this corporation shall be your church name, your city, and your state.

ARTICLE II
PURPOSE

The purpose of the church corporation shall be to establish a nonprofit, Christian religious organization to spread the gospel of Christ Jesus. The corporation will also offer the finest privileges and the fullest opportunities to the community for the Christian, religious, social, educational, and recreational good of all. The corporation will also seek to interpret the life of Christ in broad sectarian terms of unselfish service, and it will offer its fullest and best fellowship without restriction to any.

ARTICLE III
GOVERNMENT

Section 1: Government
The government of this church shall be vested in the body of believers who comprise it and whose majority vote is final. The church is subject to no other ecclesiastical body. It acknowledges

Jesus Christ as the only Lord and receives the Bible as its supreme guide in matters of faith, order, and discipline.

Section 2: Policy
This church, while having complete control over its own affairs in the light of the scriptures, recognizes the obligations and privileges of the fellowship of sister churches of like faith, order, and discipline by voluntary cooperation in missionary and other beneficial endeavors.

ARTICLE IV
MEMBERSHIP

Section 1: Directions
This church shall be guided and directed by its pastor in all spiritual and disciplinary matters as set forth by the Holy Bible. A direct line of communication shall always be available between each member of the congregation and the pastor. Membership in and relationship to the church shall be entered into, maintained, and governed by the teachings of the Holy Bible as interpreted as the inerrant Word of God by the church.

Section 2: Qualifications
This membership shall consist of persons who profess to be saved by grace through repentance toward God and faith in the Lord Jesus Christ. They must also have been immersed (baptized in water) by the authority of the church upon their profession of faith. Furthermore, they must agree to be governed by all rules, regulations, polity, and Bible doctrines as adopted by the church—namely the Eighteen Articles of Faith, which are made a part of the document, method, and guidelines.

Section 3: Admission
Each petitioning person may be received by letter of recommendation from another church of the same faith and order. Each petitioner may also be received by statement of their faith and Christian experience provided that they have been a member of a denomination of like faith and order and who, because of peculiar circumstances, have no letter.

Section 4: Orientation

Each petitioning person must enroll in the New Members' Orientation Class for instruction about Bible doctrine and the method and lifestyle of membership in the church. Upon completion of orientation, said person will be extended membership and the right hand of fellowship by the senior pastor. He or she is now a full member of the church with all the rights that accompany church membership (Matt. 28:18–20; 2 Tim. 2:15).

Section 5: Active Members

Active church members are those members who are considered in good and regular standing. They continually support the work of the church fellowship by donating their time in worship and service, their treasury to support the total gospel ministry, and their talents to advance the work of the kingdom.

Section 6: Inactive Membership

Inactive status defines a member who has not attended worship services, financially supported the total ministry of the church, nor given himself or herself in committed ministry for the growth of the kingdom for at least three months (Hebrews 10:25).

If said person has not shown activity in the above areas within the past three months, such person is considered out of fellowship with the local church body and must be restored publicly.

If said person has not given a satisfactory reason for his or her apathy (Heb. 13:17) after three months, the person will be contacted at his or her last known address. The person will be warned as well as encouraged to rectify his or her waywardness. After six months, the person's name shall be removed from the church's membership list without further contact (1 Tim. 6:1–5).

Section 7: Exclusion From Membership

Persons who have been excluded from membership may be restored to membership by coming forward at the invitation of the clergy at a public worship service. They must confess the error of their ways, ask forgiveness of the Lord Christ, apologize to the local church body, and accept direction from the senior pastor.

Section 8: Dismissal

Members may be dismissed by letter of recommendation to the

fellowship of another church of like faith and order upon action of their previous church.

The names of members who join a church of a different faith shall automatically be dropped from the church roll.

Section 9: Grievances

A. All cases of grievance between members shall be dealt with in accordance with the rules laid down in Matthew chapter 18, and no public complaint shall be heard until this course has been pursued.

B. If one or more members, in violation of a grievance, adhere not to the polity of this church as presented by the teaching of the Holy Bible, then the right hand of fellowship shall be withdrawn based on scriptural teachings (Rom. 16:17; 2 Thess. 3:10, 14).

C. No member of the church shall at any time bring suit upon this corporation in a court proceeding; any attempt by a member or a faction of members qualifies for immediate expulsion from this church. This is based on the Holy Bible's teachings (1 Cor. 6:1–6).

ARTICLE V
OFFICERS

Section 1: Officers

The officers of this corporation shall be the president who is the pastor, the chairman of the board of deacons, the administrative secretary, the business office manager, the financial secretary, the church clerk, and the treasurer.

Section 2: Qualifications

All officers must be members in good standing with this church who exhibit good stewardship practices in the areas of time, talent, and treasure. They must exemplify concern for the church physically, spiritually, and financially. The pastor shall be responsible for the general oversight of the work of the church, and shall be ex officio member of all boards or committees. He will be moderator at all the church's family meetings (business meetings).

Section 3: Judiciary Actions

No officer of this corporation shall at any time bring suit upon this corporation or its pastor. Any attempt of this kind by any officer qualifies for immediate expulsion from this corporation. This is based on the Holy Bible's teachings (1 Cor. 6:1–6).

Section 4: Duties
A.   Chairman of the Board of Deacons: The chairman shall preside at the meeting of the Board of Deacons. The vice chairman will assume the responsibilities of the chairman in the chairman's absence. In the absence of the chairman and the vice chairman, the pastor and the board of deacons shall select a deacon to act in their place.
B.   Church Clerk: The church clerk shall keep a true and correct record of the proceeding of the church, keep a record of all members, conduct the correspondence of the church, and keep all papers and documents of the church, unless otherwise ordered by the pastor.
C.   Treasurer and Financial Secretary: The treasurer is responsible for the deposit of all the church's money. The financial secretary shall pay out church money upon the instruction of the church; checks will be issued under the name of the church and cosigned by the financial secretary and treasurer. The pastor may serve as an alternate signer in the absence of one of the two.
D.   Business Office Manager: The business office manager shall keep a set of accounts covering all income and expenditures. This person will chair the budget committee in preparing a budget goal for the church for each forthcoming year. The budget will be based on anticipated income and expenditures.
E.   Administrative Secretary: The administrative secretary is responsible for all administrative duties. The administrative secretary shall work closely with the pastor and shall be appointed by the pastor.

Section 5: Officers and Ministry Leaders
All officers and ministry leaders will be appointed by the pastor upon ratification by the church body at the Annual Family Meeting (the annual business meeting) at the end of the fiscal year.

ARTICLE VI
STAFF

Section 1: Ministerial Staff
Staff Policy
A. The staff: The ministerial staff shall consist of the pastor and asso-
    ciate ministers. The pastor shall be called to the church as per the
    church's constitution and bylaws. The associate minister(s) shall
    function upon the recommendation of the pastor.
B. Salary: The pastor shall be supported by full benefits, expense
    allowance, and compensated through pastoral support via the
    church membership (Gal. 6:6; 1 Cor. 9:13, 14). An active Pastor's
    Esteem Counsel shall also be provided.
C. Other fringe benefits: The church shall provide and furnish a
    dwelling place and utilities for the pastor and his family, organize an
    annual appreciation service, and assist the pastor in his future edu-
    cation endeavors designed to better his ministry (1 Cor 9:1–14).

Section 2: Secretarial Staff
A. The Secretarial Staff shall consist of the administrative secretary,
    the financial secretary, and other secretaries as are deemed neces-
    sary. Those working part time or more shall be eligible for vacation
    and sick leave benefits. After working twelve consecutive months,
    secretaries shall be eligible for two weeks' vacation with pay. Vaca-
    tions shall be granted on a calendar year basis but must be coordi-
    nated with the pastor. After five years of continuous service, three
    weeks' vacation with pay shall be granted each year.
B. Sick Leave: After twelve consecutive months of employment, the
    equivalent of five days' sick leave will be grated each year.
C. Medical Benefits: Medical coverage shall be offered to full-time
    secretarial staff only.

Section 3: Maintenance
The maintenance staff shall consist of custodial and maintenance
help for the church buildings and grounds.
A. Vacations: After working twelve consecutive months, the mainte-
    nance staff is eligible for two weeks' vacation with pay. Vacations
    shall be granted on a calendar basis, but must be coordinated with
    the pastor. After five years of continuous service, three weeks'
    vacation with pay shall be granted each year.
B. Sick Leave: After twelve consecutive months of employment, the
    equivalent of five days' sick leave will be granted each year. This
    time is to be used for sick leave purposes only.

ARTICLE VII
MEETINGS

Section 1: Types

A. The Annual Family Meeting: This annual business meeting will be held each December. All written reports of the year's activities shall be presented at this meeting.

B. Special Meetings: Special meetings shall be called by the pastor and the Board of Deacons. Public notice shall be given from the pulpit one week in advance, stating in general terms the business to be transacted. All business to go before the church must first be presented to the pastor and deacons. If necessary, they will place the matter on the agenda for the meeting.

C. Board of Deacons: Members desiring to present an item to the Board of Deacons may do so by contacting the chairman of the Board of Deacons at least one week prior to a regular meeting. This person must indicate the subject to be presented and request permission for it to be added to the agenda.

D. Staff Meeting: Staff meetings shall be held at least once per quarter and more often if so deemed necessary by the pastor. These meetings are comprised of department leaders, auxiliary presidents, committee chairpersons, and office staff who meet with the pastor and deacons.

Section 2: Quorum and Vote

Type of Meeting	Quorum	Voting Required
Annual	10 percent of voting membership	Majority present
Special Meeting	10 percent of voting membership	Majority present
Board of Deacons	Two-thirds of deacons ministry	Majority present
Calling of a pastor	20 percent of voting membership	Two-thirds majority present

ARTICLE VIII
CHURCH YEAR

The church fiscal year shall correspond with the calendar year.

ARTICLE IX
RULES OF ORDER

"Robert's Rules of Order" as last revised shall be the parliamentary manual for the church.

ARTICLE X
AMENDMENTS

This constitution or bylaws may be amended or changed at any regular Family Meeting of the church by a majority of *good standing* members providing such amendment or change is not subversive to or in violation of the spirit and purpose of this constitution. Written notice of such change or amendment shall be read at the Family (Business) Meeting one month prior and filed with the clerk of the church no more than two succeeding Sundays preceding the vote.

Chapter 6

Back to the Basics: Stewardship of Ministry

Getting back to the basics also includes getting back to instructing the church about the stewardship of ministry, using the holistic approach. It is obvious that this means we must begin by equipping the leadership to lead. Much of the crises in many African American churches are centered on unqualified leaders.

Equipping the Leadership to Lead

Why is it important to equip the lay leadership of the church? Melvin Amerson, in his book *Stewardship in African-American Churches: A New Paradigm,* assesses the need in this manner. He writes:

> The role of leadership is vitally important in the life of any organization. Often, leadership in the church is pastor-centered, and sometimes the church depends too much upon the pastor. However, the church consists of many leaders. These leaders are not limited to persons who hold offices. Leaders are persons whom others respect, and from whom they seek their guidance."[1]

Interestingly, religious researchers George Barna and Harry R. Jackson Jr. maintain that, as a group, African American churches are the strongest culturally in the area of team-based leadership.[2] Highly effective pastors understand and acknowledge the spiritual gifts and skills of their ministry leaders and allow them to use their gifts accordingly. In numerous African American churches, the pastor

1   Amerson, 33.
2   Barna and Jackson, 56.

casts the vision and one of his primary tasks centers on transmitting this vision to his leaders so that they develop a similar passion for the work of ministry (shared ministry) required to achieve the vision.

Crucial to maintaining the proper balance and order in this idea of shared ministry is the desire and the willingness of leaders to understand and accept the parameters of the pastor/teacher. Likewise, a pastor must appropriately control his ego and affirm his leaders when apportioning stewardship to those who are serving with him. As the pastor teaches the team concept of shared ministry, good followers should become leaders who function properly in their respective roles. This collaborative effort prevents the void in the work of ministry that plagues so many churches and allows the pastor to focus upon oversight of all the ministries within the church. As a result, the church exhibits vibrant life and dynamic productivity.

Holistic stewardship as taught in the New Testament not only speaks to the individual's responsibility to manage the whole that has been entrusted to one's care, but collectively, in terms of leadership in the local church. It centers on a team, shared-ministry concept. Jesus teaches us this concept in choosing the twelve disciples whom he taught and trained, including one who would eventually betray him. But later, at the inception of the infant church, we witness the other eleven working as a team using their training as leaders to preach, teach, heal, and turn the world upside down.

Building an effective stewardship church calls for teaching and training leaders the holistic nature of the team player concept. Pastors must surround themselves with good leaders. Allow any breakdown in this area, and stewardship crisis conditions are likely to occur. As the African American church unquestionably faces stewardship challenges in the dawning years of the twenty-first century, many pastors are sensing the need for training their leaders in holistic principles of Christian stewardship. I contend that if there is breakdown or crisis in any facet of leadership, getting back to boot camp training, or getting back to the basics, is the solution to the crisis.

Back to the Basics: Equipping Leaders to Lead (A Sample Lesson Outline)

As each one has received a gift, minister it to one another, as good stewards of the manifold grace of God.

1 Peter 4:10 (NKJV)

This suggestive skeleton outline can serve as a challenge to ministry leaders who serve with their pastor, performing the work of ministry.

- » What does the word "ministry" mean?
- » What do the words "to serve" suggest?
- » What does it mean to be a ministry leader?
- » What does it mean to lead?
- » What are two elements ministry leaders must understand?

I. Leaders must understand they are appointed to serve as servants—not develop into stars.
   A. Leaders are to understand that they serve:
      1. Christ
      2. With Christ's pastor
      3. Christ's church (congregation)
   B. Leaders are to understand that their ministry is never to resemble a solo act; they are a team member who functions within the framework of a team player's concept.
   C. A successful team is always structured and functions according to the spirit of oneness.

II. Leaders must also understand the stewardship nature and element in leading a ministry.
   A. Leading a ministry calls for a sacrifice of one's time.
   B. Leadership calls on a person to shape his or her abilities to lead by using their spiritual gift.
      1. Leaders know and accept the responsibility of sharing their possessions to finance the work of the ministry and support their pastor financially.

2. Leaders are to be aware that we live in an age where marketing is the key to distribution of information. Marketing ministries is vital to today's contemporary church. Congregants of your church and visitors should know what your ministries are about.

How to Write a Format for a Ministry and a Design for a Ministry Brochure

» Assemble a team of five to six people to develop the format (the structure and an organizational flow chart for the ministry).
» Meet for input. Pray for guidance.
» Understand the ministry's purpose.
  1. Serve Christ
  2. Serve with Christ's pastor
  3. Serve Christ's people (the congregation)
» Understand why this ministry is needed.
» List these in detail:
  1. Mission Statement. It should be one sentence describing the purpose of your ministry.
  2. Vision Statement (goals)
  3. Criteria for workers

Your ministry's introduction should include an explanation of how your ministry works within the ministry of the whole church. It should also include how the ministry will be used to edify the body of Christ, as well as how it will function within the framework of the team players' concept.

A brochure should be designed introducing and detailing the ministry.

1. It should be visually attractive.
2. It should be a concise description of the particular ministry.
3. It should include photographs of your pastor and pastor's spouse, ministry director or coordinator, and staff workers.
4. It should introduce others to specific ministries and inform them what a particular ministry is all about.

5. It should seek advice from other ministry directors who have put together ministry brochures.

Conclusion: When all ministries are functioning within the framework of a team player's concept, then the African American church can experience dynamic effective leadership in the body.

Edifying the Membership to Do Ministry

Unquestionably, the primary stewardship mission of Christ's church on earth is to evangelize. According to Matthew 28:19, believers are commanded to witness to the unsaved and develop disciples of all nations. One of the most overwhelming challenges for many pastors is motivating members to share their faith with the unsaved. Yet, it is apparent that holistic stewardship without the evangelism/discipleship process would indelibly leave us without a foundation. The local church has a stewardship that must return to its holistic roots.

R. Scott Rodin in his book, *Stewards in the Kingdom,* affirms this:

> …the church's call includes the responsibility to train up disciples. The church is called to be the place where Christians can be fed by the Word of God, challenged in their walk with Christ, and encouraged in their commitment to joyful Christian obedience. It must therefore be the place where the Bible is taught, where discipleship is the goal for all Christian education, where knowledge is passed on, where open discussion can take place and where spiritual growth is nurtured and experienced. The church, as the priesthood of all believers, has a stewardship responsibility for all of the people in its local expression. The church is a faithful steward when it takes with the utmost seriousness the responsibility to make disciples of all nations, beginning with Jerusalem.[3]

According to Barna and Jackson's research, African Americans consistently demonstrate high evangelistic activity. A 2004 study revealed that nearly two-thirds of born-again black adults had shared their faith with a non-Christian in the previous year. This statistic was 30 percent higher than it was among non-black born-again adults.[4]

3 R. Scott Rodin, 182.
4 Barna and Jackson, 113.

Clearly, evangelism is an area of ministry that the African American community values and focuses upon. The evangelism-oriented pastor often presents various methods of sharing the gospel through evangelistic training programs or events, but he is careful to train members to become knowledgeable and effective witnesses. The late African American pastor Tom Skinner described it this way: "If we (pastors) are going to evangelize our communities, we must develop those who are going to communicate the good news."[5]

Effective stewards, then, are those who are involved in a discipleship process that helps them identify, develop, and ultimately utilize their spiritual gifts, which empowers them to do the real work of ministry. Every believer is endowed with at least one gift that the Holy Spirit gives according to His sovereignty. These gifts are for ministry and are meant to edify the body of Christ; and each individual as a member of the body ought to exercise appropriate stewardship of the grace gifts received.

Believers who fail to identify, strengthen, and exercise their gifts in ministry contribute to the shortage-of-workers crisis that afflicts numerous African American churches. Some have no idea of the gifts they possess, so they cannot possibly use them. Others may have identified their gifts but refuse, for various reasons, to commit them to the Lord's service. This problem can render the church ineffectual and powerless in the areas of evangelism and ministry. It is absolutely necessary that believers who are being discipled realize the importance of their gifts to the local church and the body of Christ at large if the church is going to be successful in its holistic stewardship endeavors in carrying out the divine mandate.

Back to the Basics: Evangelism and Discipleship Ministry Format

And Jesus came and spoke to them saying, "All authority has been given to me in heaven and on earth. Go therefore and make disciples of all the nations, baptizing them in the name of the Father and of the Son and of the Holy Spirit, teaching them to observe all things that I have commanded you; and lo, I am with you always even to the end of the age" (Matt. 28:18–20).

5   Ibid., 124.

This church evangelism and discipleship ministry finds its purpose and its ultimate objective, as defined in instructions given to the church by the Lord Jesus Christ, more commonly recognized as the Great Commission, "Go therefore and make disciples of all nations." Since our commission from the Lord Jesus is multifaceted, then it is imperative that our ministry be multifaceted in order to adequately address the needs of those we serve.

We exist to reach those who are lost, comfort those who are disheartened, encourage those who are discouraged, walk beside those who are weak, exhort those who are strong, teach those who are eager, help those who are helpless, direct those who are wayward, be an example for those who are young, and strive to instill the attitude of love in all who are members of this church and to those we come in contact with. This church's attitude is to always say yes to Jesus. Our goal is that this church might become a contagious church in its effectiveness in outreach, its celebration in worship, and its participation in ministry for the Lord Jesus Christ.

In order for the evangelism and discipleship ministry goals to become realities, we must catch the holistic vision of our pastor and incorporate the six steps for successful ministry as a platform for operation. Those six steps are:

1. We must plan.
2. We must prepare.
3. We must pray.
4. We must proceed.
5. We must persevere.
6. And finally, we must look to God to *perform* the vision through us.

The Plan

Our plan is to involve the entire church body in a stewardship process of evangelism and discipleship.

Our Mission Statement

We are a community of baptized believers in Christ Jesus, serving with Christ's pastor through evangelizing the lost, developing disciples, and reaching out to those in our homes, our communities, and surrounding areas.

Our Vision

I. Evangelism (Acts 1:8)
   A. Focus: Our Homes—our desire is for the entire family/household of every church member to worship together
      1. Family profile for each member of the church (your church name here)
      2. Family emphasis weekend
      3. Find out how we can serve you
      4. Relay/receive information to/from other ministries
      5. Hold each ministry accountable
   B. Focus: Our Extended Families (unsaved, non-churchgoing relatives who live outside of the household)
   C. Focus: Our Communities
      1. Street witnessing: Target areas by membership identification, demographic searches, and pastoral/ministry input. Set specific dates for street witnessing such as the Saturdays before the first and third Sunday of each month.
      2. Meet-your-neighbor campaign
   D. Focus: The Surrounding Areas

II. Discipleship (Acts 2:41–47)
   A. Focus: New Members
      1. Counseling session (regarding spiritual status and membership)
      2. Orientation: CBT (Christian basic training) is a twenty-six-week training program with an assigned disciple trainer. The disciple trainer also remains responsible for new member for one year.
      3. Discipleship training: new members will be assigned to discipleship training in pastor's class for a minimum of one year.
      4. Follow-up Home Visit: A member of the follow-up ministry team will be responsible for scheduling home

visits and following up with new members for six months.

5. Personal involvement: the person who invited the new member should remain personally involved in the new member's membership.

6. Identify and address the needs of each new member and their family: this can include home visits, discipleship interaction, and phone calls.

B. Focus: Members whose attendance is not consistent

1. Identify and address the problem; initial contact made by telephoning a team member

2. Schedule follow-up ministry contact

3. Implementation of the Excuse Elimination Program (EEP)

  » Carpool: when necessary, recruit members in various areas who will pick up those in need of transportation in their local area.

  » Childcare: Provide homework supervision and assistance for school-age children and activities for pre-school-age children. Also provide some type of meal for parents and children who do not have an opportunity to stop at home before Bible study. Parents must register ahead of time with a ministry member or the church office.

  » Be willing to address other needs as they present themselves.

C. Focus: MIA (missing in action) or those who have been missing without correspondence with the church office

1. Telephone contact (via telephony ministry from compiled list)

2. Written correspondence

3. Contact follow-up ministry team member

D. Focus: New Recruits

1. Visitors: Identify church visitors from visitor cards, and compile a contact list. Contact visitors via telephone, and send out correspondence.

2. Street witnessing: Compile contact lists from contact

sheets. Contact via telephone, send correspondence, and schedule home visitation via follow-up ministry.

3. Use the Internet: make use of Web site and e-mail system as contact resources.

III. Outreach (Matt. 9:35–38)
   A. Family emphasis weekend
   B. Meet-your-neighbor campaign
   C. Black History Parade
   D. Community fair outing
   E. Coordinate outreach dates with youth ministry
   F. Evangelism Emphasis Week (this is subject to pastoral approval)
   G. Be flexible and willing to attend new events as they are made available

IV. Criteria for team workers including counselors, disciples' follow-up team, and evangelism/discipleship ministry team members
   A. Attend church on a regular basis
   B. Be FAT (faithful, available, and teachable)
   C. Support your pastor
   D. Love saints
   E. Hunger to save lost souls
   F. Be a student of God's Word
   G. Tithe and be a cheerful giver
   H. Be willing to serve
   I. Be accountable to your area of responsibility

Educating the New Member

Why is it important to educate the new member? First of all, the new member is experiencing a new way of life that is opposite of the life lived prior to surrendering one's will to the Lordship of Christ. There are new demands being put on this person that may be confusing and breed frustrations that can only be dealt with in a teaching, question-and-answer setting. Educating the new member means systematically teaching the fundamentals of holistic stewardship, which provides the spiritual nurture and nourishments necessary for every aspect of one's Christian life.

Education includes both teaching and training. Teaching provides a plan and a path for the new member to follow while discovering the importance of a life of stewardship and total surrendering to the commands of Christ daily. It also answers questions posed by the new member that can only be answered from a scriptural basis in a teaching setting. But now, training instructs the new member how to implement stewardship principles using daily practical applications.

Why is educating the new member important? It is important because the timing is ideal for a teacher and the new member who is opened to learning new stewardship principles.

George E. Brazell has this say about new members' training:

> Any growing church will be receiving new members continually. Even before they become an official part of the church family, these people should understand that being a Christian is both a privilege and a responsibility. This includes adopting the practice of Christian stewardship because a faithful follower of Jesus will abide by all his teachings. New members should be taught to support the church with their three basic possessions: finance, time, and abilities. If they learn to give to the Lord in every respect, they will be a spiritual treasure to the church.[6]

Getting back to the basics and teaching holistic stewardship of biblical principles also means beginning with the basics. The basics must begin with each new member. If not, the stewardship crisis in the African American church will continue to perpetuate.

See Appendix B, "Suggestive Tools for New Membership Training."

---

6   George E. Brazell, *Dynamic Stewardship Strategies: Harnessing Time, Talent, and Treasury for Church Growth* (Grand Rapids: Baker Book House, 1989), 80–81.

Chapter 7

Back to the Basics: Stewardship of Money

Financing the Church Ministry

In my opinion, much of the financial stewardship crisis that inflicts the typical African American church is derived from the fact that there are too many debt-ridden Christians who have been lured by the temptation of deceit and greed. The problem continues to perpetuate, and the crisis is apparent. Debt-ridden Christians end up becoming deadbeat stewards.

Is there something the church can do? I propose that teaching holistic stewardship is the answer to correcting the crisis. Because of intensifying budget demands and the financial crises churches face today, most pastors spend their time and energy teaching and preaching about the stewardship of money matters. However, I suggest that before we can deal efficiently with money matters, we must first deal with this question: what's wrong with our members? Holistic stewardship covers the totality of one's Christian's lifestyle, not just sections of one's Christian walk.

Debt is an addiction. Any addiction is the result of a choice; you chose to be lured by some means of temptation. A proverb in the Old Testament advises us that "the rich rules over the poor, and the borrower is servant to the lender."[1]

Dr. Richard A. Swenson, in his book *The Overload Syndrome: Learning to Live Within Your Limits*, states the following in his chapter on choices and decisions:

Many people bemoan how trapped they are in life; the boss expects

---

1   Proverbs 22:7 (NKJV).

too much, the family demands too much, the debts mounts [sic] too fast. But ultimately, we live in a world of our own choosing; this is true even if we do not feel like the choice is ours.[2]

Debt is serious and has become an enormous problem in our society. Many members in our churches struggle financially as a result of debt; and what affects the home will ultimately have an effect on the local church. I propose that teaching members how to get out of debt, and how to stay out of debt, is just as important as teaching them to become generous givers.

Back to the Basics: Digging out of Debt
Sample Lesson 1

The rich rules over the poor, and the borrower is servant to the lender.

Proverbs 22:7

What is debt?

Debt is the result of the inability to meet an agreed-upon contract.

If a person buys something on credit, that is not necessarily debt. It is a contract. However, when the terms of that contract are violated because of the inability to fulfill the contract, then debt occurs.

What does a contract consist of?
1. The amount of repayment
2. The period (monthly) for repayment
3. The time to complete the repayment

Debt occurs the minute the borrower is unable to meet any one of these obligations

What about our mindset toward debt?

When one continues to borrow without means to repay, it is sug-

---

2   Richard A. Swenson, MD. *The Overload Syndrome: Learning to Live Within Your Limits* (Colorado Springs: NavPress, 1999), 95.

gested that the mindset has fallen into an attitude of deceit and greed (cf. Prov. 22:7; 1 Tim. 6:10–15).

Do not miss this point. Financial bondage begins with an attitude, not a lack of money (cf. Ps. 37:21; 112:5; Matt. 6:19–21).

Symptoms of debt
1. Overdue bills
2. Investment worries
3. Savings and assets that interfere with our Christian financial responsibilities
4. Interest in get-rich-quick schemes (cf. Prov. 10:22)
5. Not being gainfully employed (cf. Titus 3:14)
6. Deceitfulness
7. Greed
8. Jealousy
9. Covetousness
10. Family needs go unmet
11. Christian needs go unmet
12. Spending too much time at work

Remember...
God's desire is that Christians be debt free (cf. Prov. 22:7). However, He also desires that we honor our contracts and pay our bills (cf. Ps. 37:21).

God's people, given the facts, will normally do the right thing.

Dealing with the Debt Trap
Sample Lesson 2

Do you not know that to whom you present yourselves slaves to obey, you are that one's slaves whom you obey...

Romans 6:16

This lesson is the result of an article I read while researching information for my dissertation. The article, written by the Rev. Samuel Atchison, came from an original article written by columnist Claude Lewis, who writes for the *Philadelphia Inquirer*. In his column, Lewis contends that African Americans waste too much money. He contends that this is particularly true among members of the black middle class. Lewis contends that blacks spend $282 billion annually.

Atchison agrees with Mr. Lewis's assertion. He (Lewis) argues that the collective dream of Black America controlling her economic destiny is imperiled by frivolous spending. I wholeheartedly agree. It's a result of debt entrapment. Mr. Lewis went on to say, "If more of that income ($282 billion in annual spending by blacks) were saved or carefully invested, it could make an enormous difference in the growth potential of African Americans all across the country."

The Problem: Too many saints are debt-ridden Christians who are entrapped by debt. They are slaves to spending rather than servants of good stewardship. The Bible teaches, "To whom you yield yourselves servants to obey, his servants you are to whom you obey" (Romans 6:16).

The Principle: What one yields to is what one is going to serve. The word "yield," from the Greek word *paristēmi*, is derived from two words. It comes from *pará* (near), and *hístēmi* (to place, stand). Together they form the word *paristēmi,* which translates as "to place oneself at the disposal of something or someone." This principle holds true regardless of race, level of education, or social status.

The Point:

» Consider drug addicts; they yield to whatever substance is controlling their conduct. They place themselves at the disposal of the drugs.
» Consider alcoholics; they yield to the alcohol that controls their actions.

The point is that the same is true for anyone who exhibits addictive behavior toward debt. Their actions may be the result of any number of symptoms, but the outcome will be the same. Whatever temptation you yield to, ultimately, that is what or whom you will serve .

What's the Application?

In many cases, too many Christians have been lured and seduced by the latest fashions and television advertisements. As a consequence of these seductions, many Christians continue to incur heightening levels of debt.

The Peril: Given the uncertain nature of the economy, downsizing in both the public and private sectors it is likely to remain a fact of life. This is the peril of debt entrapment. To anyone living from paycheck to paycheck, the loss of a job could prove to be a financial fatality.

Is there a strategy we can use to deal with the debt trap?

Yes. Overcoming the addiction of spending that leads to debt entrapment begins with the following:

1. Confess that your debt is an addiction. Many people are slaves to debt.

When debt becomes your master, God is no longer in control of your finances. Thus, the person who is a slave to debt is not in God's will (Prov. 22:7; Matt. 6:24; 33).

2. Consecrate God's money back to Him.

1 Chronicles 29:14 says, in part, "All things come of Thee, and of Thine own have we given Thee."

This prayer should serve as an offertory prayer in every church and as a prayer in every Christian home because it reflects a valuable truth regarding God's ownership of our finances and our responsibility to use them for Him as His stewards.

3. Consider living on a budget.

"Be diligent to know the state of your flocks [affairs]" (Proverbs 27:23).

Your budget should be based on actual income and expenses. In developing a budget, priority should be given to whom or what is most important.

4. Pay the tithe first.

Proverbs 3:9 states, Honor the Lord with your possessions, and with the first fruits of all your increase.

The word "honor," in this instance, means "to give weight." In other words, prioritize in terms of importance. Consider God first in the allocation of your finances. Remember that the tithe (the first 10 percent of one's income) belongs to Him.

5.   Pay yourself second (saving/investments plan)

Remember, the bills will always be there, but the money may not.

Thus, the second 10 percent of your income should be set aside for savings.

Compare Proverbs 6:6–8, the parable of the ant, and Proverbs 21:20, the dealing of a wise man.

Saving/Investments Plan
(This should be a "do-not-touch" account)

Examples:

$150	x	52	=	$7,800	x		3 yrs	=	$23,400
					x		5 yrs	=	$39,000
$100	x	52	=	$5,200	x		3 yrs	=	$15,600
							5 yrs	=	$26,000
$50	x	52	=	$2,600	x		3 yrs	=	$7,800
							5 yrs	=	$13,000
$25	x	52	=	$1,300	x		3 yrs	=	$3,900
							5 yrs	=	$6,500

Start somewhere; pay yourself!
6.   Prioritize your bills.

Only you can determine which bills are most important, but here is a good rule of thumb. Pay those bills first that are necessary for you to survive: your home, your car, utilities, etc.

7. Pay something on each debt every month.

8. Keep records of your payments.

Keep good records of each bill you pay (Proverbs 24:30–34).

Make sure you record the date, the name of creditor, and the amount you paid.

Keep in mind that you didn't get in debt overnight, and you probably won't get out of debt overnight. But if you remain consistent, God will honor your efforts.

It is important to remember, given the facts, God's people will normally do the right thing.

Family Finances
(Sample Lesson 3)

Keep your lives free from the love of money and be content with what you have, because God has said, "never will I leave you; never will I forsake you."

Heb. 13:5

The Smiths' marriage was near the breaking point. John was tense and not smiling. Sandra was red-eyed with mascara streaked down her face as she sat stiffly in my office. I led our counseling session off with a brief prayer; then I asked John to tell me about their problems.

With a defensive edge in his voice, John said, "Sandra don't like the way I handle our finances. I admit we have problems, but with a little more time and cooperation, I could—"

Sandra interrupted, her voice raised, and her speech accelerated. "A little more time? You always say that! You've been saying that for too long. You know our phone has been disconnected three times this year already. You've been telling people we *sold* our Cadillac. Please tell the truth. It was repossessed three months ago. We're always behind on our mortgage. We have only seven days to pay our electric bill before the service is turned off. And we don't even *have* a savings account."

After a few seconds, John started in. "You know very well I had to use most of my last paycheck to pay overdue bills and credit card minimums. If you got a job, maybe it would release some of the pressure and the load."

Sandra replied, "I had a job, but you made me quit—remember? It was not working out. We were paying too much for childcare. Your words were, and I quote, 'I want you to stay home and take care of the kids. I can manage.' Please, John, make up your mind."

Raising his voice, John uttered, "Woman, be careful."

Turning to me, John softened his voice a bit. "I told Sandra I could take care of our finances, but she insisted we should come to you. I really don't see how you can help us. I keep telling Sandra I can do it."

Sparks flew from Sandra's eyes as she began to rant, "It's the same old thing, John, and I am not buying it anymore! Why not admit it? You're too proud to let anyone know we're in trouble." John stared at the floor as if he were boring two holes in it with his eyes.

Finally, I spoke softly and cautioned both of them to take it easy. "The Lord has handled tougher problems than yours. I'm sure His wisdom from His Word can resolve the tension between the two of you, as well as your family finances."

The scenario you just read is a typical, modern-day case study. The scene is so familiar because money problems inevitably spell marital problems. Let's use this case study to see if we can provide a dialogue and highlight the underlying reasons for their problems.

As it is a typical scene for many of us, we will be able to detect our own family financial mess. Obviously, this couple had arrived at a mutually destructive standoff. The reason for this was that each person had built-up resentment for their spouse.

When fueled by the frustration of a financial mess, resentment can build beneath the surface of a marriage. In some cases the resentment is noticeable. For example, a wife who was once loving and soft-spoken may become a hard-nosed, loudmouthed nag. Resentment is also often noticed in a wife who is simply tired of the family debt crises.

However, a husband who is lacking in understanding and is confused by his God-given role as head of the household can create a financial mess. He may have inadequate skills in the area of finances, but biblically he holds headship over his wife and family (1 Cor. 11:3;

Eph. 5:23). However, the family unit is one (Eph. 5:31). He and his wife are also a team. Headship here refers to leadership in the home. But be cautioned, these sayings imply responsibility, not invulnerability.

Commentary: Husbands are not immune to weaknesses or inadequacy. Do not let pride keep your finances in a mess. God gave you a "helpmate." Let her help you (Gen. 2:20; Prov. 18:22).

The couple in this scenario had conflicting attitudes about money. The first principle this couple needed to remember is that all we have belongs to God, and he wants us to use it wisely. Our attitude toward money can block our relationship with God. The rich young ruler in Luke 18:18–25 and Ecclesiastes 5:10 is an example. Perhaps the husband in our story did not understand that having the right attitude toward money also includes making wise investments and saving (Prov. 21:20; Matt. 25:14–30). Perhaps the wife's attitude was formulated by her desire to remain on par with her friends. She could have been competing with the Joneses on a number of playing fields:

1. She wanted to have a car like the Joneses'.
2. She wanted a house as big and beautiful as the Joneses'.
3. She wanted clothes that were as nice as or better than Mrs. Jones's.

This type of competition can lead to debt (cf. Proverbs. 22:7; Luke 12:15; I Tim. 6:6–9).

Perhaps this couple was lacking knowledge of biblical guidelines in reference to money. As is the case with many who fall into debt, the problem is not income. Impulsive spending and overspending are symptoms of the problem. The truth of the matter is that husbands and wives need to develop their attitudes under God's authority and follow scriptural guidelines when it comes to handling money. The challenge will be *The Word vs. the world.*

Note: As a Christian family, what does it do to your witness if you are always living beyond your means? Are you always late paying bills? Are you always juggling from one month to the next? Are you getting payments in just ahead of the collection agency's phone calls?

If this is your situation, I suggest you are under indictment before

the Lord because of bad stewardship. Perhaps it is time to bring your
finances under biblical guidelines.

I suggest several things to consider:

I. Know where your money comes from.
    A. It is God who is responsible for our wealth (Deut. 8:18; Prov.
       10:22).
    B. God does not want us to trust in our wealth, nor be con-
       ceited, but to give and share (1 Tim. 6:17–19).

II. Know where your money is going.
    A. How and where are you spending your money?
    B. How do you determine how you will allocate your income?

III. Suggestions on how to keep track of where your money is
     going:
    A. Start a journal.
    B. Write down each purchase you make over the course of a
       month.
    C. Add bills that are not payable monthly (like semi-annual or
       quarterly insurance premiums). Add a monthly figure for
       those, as well.

IV. Three categories you should consider:
    A. Fixed Expenses:
       1. Tithes and offering (minister and ministry)
       2. Savings
       3. Mortgage/rent
       4. Automobile
       5. Property taxes
       6. Insurance
       7. Debts (take charge of those credit cards; this may mean
          cutting them up)
    B. Variable Expenses:
       1. Food
       2. Utilities
       3. Medical/dental

    4. Clothing
    5. Maintenance
  C. Discretionary Expenses
    1. Entertainment
    2. Miscellaneous

Note: Don't miss this!

Why is it necessary to start with a journal that lets you know where your money is being spent? Many couples charge purchases faster than they can pay them off. It is common that either the wife is an impulsive spender or the husband is. In many cases, both are. Many of us handle our finances without a schedule; there is no flight plan. As a result, we end up flying blind. Few of us are able to say, "We can't afford it," and walk away. This suggests a real shortage of self-discipline.

It's time to start.

Begin to uncover your problem areas.

Here's how:

1. Compare your spending habits with a suggested budget.
2. Make positive changes in your spending.
3. Use your budget to create your plan.
4. Give (Luke 6:38; 2 Cor. 9:6–10). Remember, God does not need your gifts as much as you need to give them (Prov. 11:24–25).
5. Keep your expenses within the bounds of your income. Stay within your budget. (Prov. 13:18).
6. Avoid debt. If you are in debt, get out as quickly as you can. If at all possible, stay out (Prov. 22:7; Rom. 13:8; 2 Pet. 2:19).

Finally, consider this practical exercise and review your situation (circle your answers).

1. My spouse and I both support the ministry and minister with tithes and offerings. Yes or No
2. I tithe, but my spouse does not. Yes or No

3. I tithe:
    » Regularly
    » Sometimes
    » Never
4. Right now I give $_____ to my church each month.
5. There is built-up resentment in my household because of my poor handling of finances. Yes or No
6. My spouse and I are in debt. Yes or No
7. I will commit $_____ extra each month to getting out of debt.
8. I realize now that I must bring my finances under God's authority. Yes or No

A PERSONAL PRAYER

"Father, forgive me. I confess my financial problem is a spiritual problem. I commit my finances under your authority. I commit to being a faithful steward over your possessions. I realize that all I have comes from you. All my needs, you are providing. All I shall give, you will guide.

"Father, I commit to the tithing principle. I will commit to worshipping you regularly, supporting my pastor, and supporting my church. I thank you for the grace of confession and forgiveness."

Amen.

Back to the Basics: Teaching the Tithing Principle

In this section, our brief analysis will be limited. Much of our discussion pertaining to tithing was based on brief research that was presented in chapter 3. Tithing provides the origin and the foundation for all Christian giving.

There has been much debate and mixed views on the concept of tithing. Some scholars contend that tithing is an Old Testament idea and that it is not commanded in the New Testament. Because of the broad nature of the subject, it is not the design of this book to continue that long line of debate. However, using limited comments, I would argue that tithing is not a concept but a stewardship principle that gives us the basis of acknowledging God's ownership of everything. The author of the book of Hebrews stated, "Jesus Christ is the same yesterday, today, and forever."[3] This speaks of Christ's immutability. *The International Standard Bible Encyclopedia* affirms Christ's immutability: "It is the perfection of Yahweh that He changes not in character, will, purpose, aim (Mal 3:6; Heb 13:8).[4]

One could argue that if God does not change, neither does his Word or principles. The responsibility of the exegete in interpreting scripture is to begin where God began and continue with the line of truth in light of its context as it proceeds to consummation. Whether the practice of tithing is an Old Testament practice and not a command for New Testament saints remains debatable.

However, in a typical African American church, the tithing principle is taught. Although many pastors and congregations only approach it from the surface, their fear is creating a stewardship syndrome. If a church is struggling to maintain financial stability and it subscribes to the tithing principle, then getting back to the basics and teaching the principle of tithing is fundamental. I contend that the problem with the tithe debate is that few people really take the time to examine the principle. Seldom is God's original purpose underscored. As a result, the practice of tithing is undermined, and the penalty is underestimated. From this author's viewpoint, the list is replete of God's promises bestowed upon those who are faithfully practicing the tithing principle.

Larry Burkett, a noted author in the area of finance, had this to say about God's promises: "Once an understanding of God's promise is reached, it is necessary to believe that promise."[5]

Suggested Lesson
Mal. 3:6-12; 1 Cor. 9:1-14

The New Testament's purpose for tithing is to finance God's work and compensate the overseer of His church.

---

3   Heb. 13:8 (NKJV).

4   Orr, J., MA, DD (1999). *The International Standard Bible Encyclopedia: 1915 edition* (J. Orr, Ed.). Albany, OR: Ages Software.

5   Larry Burkett. *Giving and Tithing: Includes Serving and Stewardship* (Chicago: Moody Press, compiled from material originally published by Christian Financial Concepts, Inc., 1991), 19.

This is a good place to start because tithing serves as the foundation for our stewardship of giving. It undergirds our discipline in obedience to the Lord.

Therefore, we must make sure we understand the principle of tithing; we must be convinced of the purpose for New Testament tithing; and we must eradicate our careless practice of sporadic tithing. If not, we will experience the penalty.

I.   The major problem is we do not take time to study and understand the principle.
     »   *Principle* is a fundamental truth or spiritual condition that explains a natural or spiritual action.
     »   *Tithe* means to pay or give a tenth part of something especially for the support of the church.
     »   The tithing principle has two components (Malachi 3:8)
         1.   Tithes
         2.   Offerings

Therefore, the tithing principle is the faithful practice of obeying God by returning the first tenth of our increase (compensation) to a place designated by God's plan. We are returning a debt we already owe. The principle also involves the giving of an offering in proportion to a person's prosperity. This is done as a presentation to God as an act of worship (Proverbs 3:9; Mal. 3:10; 1 Corinthians 16:1–2; 2 Corinthians 9:6–10). Where is that place today for New Testament Saints? It is the local church.

Let's examine scripture in view of today's controversy concerning tithing.

   A.   Some say tithing is not for New Testament saints. They say it was for those who lived under the Mosaic Law. However, Genesis 14:20 and Genesis 28:22, as alluded to in chapter 3, teach that tithing was being practiced before the law. One should note that Abram/Abraham had to have lived some four hundred years before the law was given to Moses.
   B.   Also, scripture teaches that the principle of tithing was continued during the time of the Mosaic Law (cf. Lev. 27:30;

Num. 18:20–24; Deut. 14:28–29; 2 Chron. 31:4–10; Neh. 12:12; Mal. 3:8–1).

C. How does the tithing principle relate to the New Testament? Did Jesus have anything to say about tithing? Did he commend or condemn it? Let's examine His Word about the subject.

Woe unto you, scribes and pharisees, hypocrites! For you pay tithes of mint and anise and cummin, and have omitted the weightier *matters* of the law: justice and mercy and faith. These ought ye have done, without leaving the other undone (Matt. 23:23).

Commentary: Jesus did not condemn the principle of tithing in this text. What he condemned was the hypocrites' priority of the practice. They were putting more emphasis on tithing than on prioritizing those things that were valued the most. It is clear that the tithing principle was still being practiced during Jesus's day.

Also, when we compare scripture with scripture in the context of Jesus's earthly mission and His father's will, we discover that Jesus never condemned anything on earth that the father, in glory, had already commanded (cf. John 1:1–3; 14; Matthew 5:17; John 5:19; 2 Corinthians 5:19; 1 Timothy 3:16).

» It is clear that the principle of tithing was conceived in the mind of God in eternity before the foundation of the world. This principle was ordained (set in place) by God before the Mosaic Law was given to Israel (cf. Gen. 14:20; Gen. 28:22).

» God is immutable. He does not change, and neither do his principles. It is God's principle for his people. Tithing is a spiritual matter, not a money matter. It is about what belongs to God.

II. Another problem is that we do not take time to study in order to understand the purpose for tithing. In order to understand God's purpose for tithing, one should begin where God first introduced a purpose (Numbers 18:20–24, 31).

Question

What was God's original purpose for the tithing principle under the Mosaic Law?

Answer

It was used to support or compensate the Levites and priests. They were God's chosen workers (spiritual leaders) under the law to oversee the spiritual operation in the congregation of the tabernacle. The tithes they received were their wages for working for God. God instituted it (cf. Num. 18:20–24; 31). Is there a purpose today? Again, remember that God's principles do not change because they are eternal. Therefore, it is safe to say that if His principles are eternal, then His purposes are eternal also.

Commentary

In interpreting scripture or seeking out truths pertaining to any subject, there is a basic rule one can take into account: scripture does not contradict itself; scripture interprets scripture. Therefore cross-referencing the following scriptures can help pinpoint God's purpose for tithing today: cf. Gen. 14:20; Gen. 28:22; Lev. 27:30–31; Num. 18:20–24; 31; Matt. 10:10; Luke 10:7; 1 Tim. 5:17–18; 1 Cor. 9:1–14; Gal. 6:6; 2 Tim. 2:6; 1 Corinthians 16:1–2; 2 Corinthians 9:6–10. From my understanding of the listed scriptures, today's purpose is twofold:

1. Financial support for the Lord's minister (cf. 1 Cor. 9:1–14 with 2 Tim. 2:6).
2. Financial support for church ministries (1 Cor. 16:1–2).

To clear up matters concerning the minister, we must look again at 1 Cor. 9:7–14. Because of Satan's deceit and the many myths (misguided lies) pertaining to the minister of a church and money, it is important to note keywords in 1 Corinthians 9:13–14.

In verse 13, the keyword is "partaker." It's renders from the Greek word *summerizomai*, which translates "to share jointly with; to divide into portions."

In verse 14, the keyword is the phrase "even so." From the Greek words *houtōs kai*, it translates "in like manner," "likewise," "the same," "just as," "so it is," or "as it was."

Don't miss this. Notice how verse 14 qualifies verse 13. "Even so the Lord hath commanded that those who preach the gospel should live from the gospel" (cf. 1 Cor. 9:13–14).

Understanding the purpose ought to help eradicate the careless practice and lead us to a spirit of obedience. If the Lord ordained it, then the people of God ought to not be afraid to practice it. Besides, there are some promised blessings (cf. 2 Chron. 31:4–10; Mal. 3:10–12; Phil. 4:19).

III. Understanding the purpose of tithing will help keep us from undermining the practice and from becoming confused.

The confusion is more prevalent when:

1. Many believe and continue to teach that tithing was a command under Israel's law.
2. They teach that New Testament saints are not under the law and, therefore, tithing is not compelled and is no longer a component for Christian giving.
3. They teach that tithing is a practice of legalism and to practice it does not express freewill giving as a result of grace.

However, biblical record teaches:

1. God *commanded* the tithing principle before the law.
2. God *continued* the tithing principle under the Mosaic law.
3. Jesus did not *condemn* the tithing principle during his earthly ministry.
4. The Apostle Paul *consummated* the principle of tithing as a principle ordained by the Lord.

Be careful of the age-old debate, old vs. new. Consider that the Old Testament conceals what the New Testament reveals. Also, the Old Testament contains what the New Testament explains. Then consider: *You can adhere to law without loving it, but when you love, the law is never the issue.* It is important to understand both principle and purpose so that you do not undermine the practice. Why?

Though some yet will be confused, they will not be excused. Those who do not practice the principle will not escape the penalty.

The Bible does not use language such as "nontither" or "inconsistent tithers." According to Malachi 3:8, the language is precise: "Will a man rob God? Yet, ye have robbed me. But ye say, 'wherein have we robbed thee?' in tithes and offerings." To not obey suggests one is a God robber. Those who are yet careless with the practice will be subject to the penalty. The penalty is severe! To be cursed literally means to hem in or bind up. It refers to a drying up of blessings. *Do not underestimate the penalty! You may be confused, but you will not be excused.*

Finally, let us be reminded that repetition is the key to learning and understanding. If your stewardship has come under fire, *you can jump-start it again!* It must be given serious attention. If not, you could be labeled a "blessing blocker" (cf. Mal. 3:8–12; Phil. 4:13–19). Remember, God is not partial with his punishment (Mal. 3:9; Col. 3:25). But now, neither is God partial with his promises.

Teaching Grace Giving

Many scholars suggest that the current method of giving for New Testament saints is what is commonly called grace giving. Many argue that the system of tithing required giving under the law. These same people argue that this system is no longer imposed because believers are now living under grace.

However, I contend several things for consideration:

» Law is not an issue when love is the basis for one's motivation. That is to say, you can adhere to law without loving it, but when you love it, law is never the issue.

» I would argue that the text used by many—2 Corinthians chapters 8 and 9—to suggest that the Apostle Paul outlined grace-giving principles governing the New Testament pattern of giving is not valid. Contextually, I contend that the text pertained to a specific event, a special aid gift for the poor saints in Jerusalem, not a general rule to replace the principle of tithing. Paul's specific order to the Corinthians' church for this specific aid sharing (partnering in fellowship) with the church in Jerusalem enlightens us more pertaining to the event.[6]

» Some suggest grace giving supplants the Old Testament principle of the tithe. However, a careful exegetical study of Christian giving teaches us that grace giving does not supplant the principle of the tithe. It surpasses it in practice. To supplant suggests, "to uproot; replace or eradicate." But now, to surpass implies "to exceed," i.e., "to become better or go beyond."

» The tithe is the starting point for all giving. But now, grace giving transcends in practice. It is grace giving that moves us to a mature level in Christian stewardship, a level that epitomizes generous giving.

Sample Lesson
The Grace of Generosity
2 Cor. Chapters 8 and 9

Introduction

Here in 2 Corinthians 8 and 9, the Apostle Paul outlines the grace principles governing the New Testament pattern of giving. Some suggest it supplants the Old Testament principle of the tithe.

However, a careful exegetical study of Christian giving teaches us that grace giving does not supplant the principle of the tithe. It surpasses in practice. To supplant means "to uproot, replace, or eradicate." To surpass implies "to exceed," i.e., "to become better or go beyond."

The tithe is our starting point. But grace giving transcends in practice. It is grace giving that moves us to a mature level in Christian stewardship, a level that epitomizes generous giving.

One of the problems the Christian church faces is immaturity in its stewardship. Too many members are undeveloped in their giving. Maturity implies that a person is fully developed or grown up. Too many Christians are babes when it comes to giving; they are selfish and self-consumed. You might deem these traits as immaturity in the "grace of generosity." Here is the point: there will be no maturity in Christian stewardship until we, as saints, master the grace of generosity.

6   1 Cor. 16:1–3 (NKJV).

A church cannot be healthy if its members are not generous givers. In fact, a church can abound in everything, but it is not ready to be called a mature or a model church until its members master the grace of generosity. To prove this, compare verse 7 of Corinthians chapter 8. It says:

But as you abound in everything—in faith, in speech, in knowledge, in all diligence, and in your love for us—see that you abound in this grace also.

In this text, we witness an example of a group of churches that obviously mastered the grace of generosity. Paul wrote of them to serve as a model for the Corinthian church. They were called the churches of Macedonia. I believe the generous spirit of these churches can still serve as a model today. Also, bear in mind, though this letter was not written to us, it was written ultimately for us (2 Tim. 3:16–17). These two chapters affirm at least five truths concerning the grace of generosity:

I. As saints we have been given the ability to give generously (verse 1).

    "Now brethren, we wish to make known to you the grace of God which has been given in the churches of Macedonia."

    A. The ability to give generously is not derived from our human nature but is a gift bestowed upon us by the grace of God.
        1. It is God's grace that becomes the power that changes us into generous givers. The credit is never ours to claim; it is always God's.
        2. God's grace can move us to generosity. It is power within us that motivates and moves us to give according to His will. God's grace can move our hearts to give generously.

    B. Generous giving is not a natural thing for us.
        1. We are more naturally takers rather than givers. We instinctively think of ourselves before others. Humans are not naturally generous.

2. Looking at creation, man is God's only creation that has a problem with giving.
    a. The sun gives light and heat.
    b. The stars give splendor.
    c. The moon gives radiance.
    d. The clouds give rain.
    e. The mountains give security.
    f. The flowers give fragrance.
    g. The grass gives beauty.
    h. The trees give fruit.
    i. The animals give meat.
    j. The earth gives minerals.
    k. The ground gives crops.
    l. The crops give food.
    m. The water gives to quench our thirst.

    Man naturally gives nothing. But God's grace can move our hearts to give generously.

II. God's grace can move our minds to think generously.
    A. The mind is the control center for our bodies.
    B. Our bodies are active expressions of our attitudes.
    C. Our behavior invariably is shaped by our beliefs (cf. Prov. 11:24–25; 1 Tim. 6:17–18).

III. God's grace can move our hands to give generously.
    A. God's grace does not prod us to give; it frees us with privilege to master generosity (v.3, "according to their ability…they were freely willing").
    B. When God moves on our hearts to give generously, He actually shows us by His grace that we can put "ability into action" (cf. verse 4).

IV. As saints we have been given the ability to give sacrificially (cf. verses 2; 3b).
    A. We can experience the grace of generosity in spite of affliction (verse 2).

B. We can experience the grace of generosity in spite of circumstances.
C. We can experience the grace of generosity in spite of financial hardships.
D. We can experience the grace of generosity even in the battles
of poverty-stricken conditions.

Note: What steps can we take in maturing in sacrificial giving?

1. Understand that sacrificial giving is a voluntary deed and
not an unpopular duty (cf. v.3; 5; 12).
2. Like the Macedonian churches, allow our reason to give
sacrificially and generously to be motivated by God's
grace.
3. Understand that the biblical practice for generosity as
witnessed in the New Testament is always twofold:
a. Sharing as a fellowship with saints in need (2 Cor. 8
and 9).
b. Sharing as a fellowship to support saints who lead (cf.
Gal. 6:6; Phil. 4:14–18; 1 Thess. 5:12–13).

V. As saints, we have the ability to give bountifully (2 Cor. 9:6–8).
A. True generosity is not only measured by how much one gives,
but is also measured by what one keeps. "But this I say: He
who sows sparingly will also reap sparingly, and he who sows
bountifully, will also reap bountifully" (2 Cor. 9:6).

Notice: The word *bountifully* in this verse does not mean much or
more. It refers to a sowing with blessing. The idea is that every time
we give, it should express our generosity by the grace of God through
unconditional love with the intent to be a blessing as a motive for our
giving.

B. True generosity is planned, purposed, and proportionate
giving (2 Cor. 9:7a).
C. True generosity is bountiful giving done with joy (2 Cor.
9:7b).

D. Finally, true generosity is bountiful giving that looks first to God's grace before giving, when giving, and after giving (2 Cor. 9:8).

What is the application?

The manner of our giving should always be determined by our motive for giving. Our motive should be to give generously because God gives so generously to us. Paul's words to the Corinthian saints were, "For you know the grace of our Lord Jesus Christ that though He was rich, yet for your sake He became poor, that you through His poverty might become rich" (2 Cor. 8:9).

Our giving should always be an expression of generosity for what God did for us through Jesus Christ. Christ is our example. He died for our sins, and through His resurrection we were justified according to faith. Saints have a new relationship with God. That is a motive for generous, sacrificial, and bountiful giving.

Therefore, let us mature in the body (fully develop) as the church of Jesus Christ demonstrating through our giving the grace of generosity. It is only then we prove the sincerity of our love. The Holy Spirit's words to us through the Apostle Paul are the same as to the Corinthian church: "But just as you abound in everything, in faith, and utterance, and knowledge and in all earnestness, and in the love we inspired in you, see that you abound in gracious work also." The grace of generosity, to God be the glory.

Financially Supporting the Lord's Minister

This book would not be complete without addressing one of the most severe crises that confronts the average African American church. Finding funds to provide financial support for the pastor is an ongoing crisis in a typical African American church. Whether it is adequate compensation or providing maintenance benefits for the Lord's full-time worker, both problems have coexisted and have created much uneasiness among pastor and people.

As stated previously, because of their financial difficulties, many church budgets limit pastors' salaries and benefits. Many churches do not provide their pastor with a medical and dental plan. Others may provide a medical plan, but no retirement plan. The other scenario is that, in many cases, pastors are forced to get a second job to supplement their income. But now, I contend the problem does not lie in finding enough funds to financially support the Lord's pastor. The problem is not the funds; it is faithfully obeying the biblical principles outlined in scripture, the biblical basis for financially supporting a pastor of a church. Teaching holistic stewardship gives us a biblical basis to use to correct the crisis.

This book recommends the biblical principle to teach. It will point out that God never calls a pastor, commissions him, and then leaves him confused as to how he should be compensated and spiritually supported. The biblical mandate has stood the test of time, and many African American pastors are leading their churches back to the basics. As a result, in many of these churches, the crisis is already being corrected.

The Old and New Testaments are satiated with evidence that God instructs His people of their stewardship obligation in financially supporting their leaders just as today, God instructs the pastor of a church of his stewardship responsibility in shepherding the church. Supporting a pastor financially is a spiritual matter, not a secular matter. Truth involving any spiritual matters should be derived from biblical principles. Therefore, I would argue, if the Bible teaches a biblical principle, then it ought to become the fundamental teaching for every church practice.

Further, as stated before, the idea that what will work in one church will not work in all churches is merely philosophical and not theological. Again, supporting a pastor financially is not a secular matter but a spiritual matter. The obeying of godly principles is not based on quantity or geography, but God's people, when given the facts, will normally do the right thing.

Teaching the Church the Biblical Basis for Compensating the Lord's Pastor
1 Corinthians 9:1–14

Suggested Lesson
By way of introduction, let me begin by saying there is much immaturity in the body of Christ (local church) when it comes to

financially supporting the Lord's pastor. The question must be asked, "Can one appreciate the ministry of the Word and not appreciate the one who ministers the Word?" Biblically, the obvious answer is no (cf. Jer. 3:15; Eph. 4:11–12; Gal.6:6).

However, many believers are unlearned or misinformed of their stewardship responsibility in supporting their soul-watcher (Heb.13:17), the Lord's overseer (Acts 20:28) of His church. But now, whether one is unlearned or misinformed, the Bible is not silent on this issue. As a matter of fact, in my opinion, any issue the Bible cannot address is not worth addressing. Therefore, because compensation for a pastor is an important issue, the Bible does address it.

Probably the most obvious question should be, if the Lord calls a pastor and commissions him, would the Lord leave him (the pastor) confused in how he is to be compensated and cared for? Scripture is clear and consistent. Even so, the Lord has commanded that those who preach the gospel should live from the gospel (1 Cor. 9:14). That is Divine Order. But now here is the problem: whenever you disturb or modify Divine Order, the outcome will be disorder and the consequence will be confusion, chaos, and ultimately compromise. What you will have is not unity but disunity.

With this in mind, I believe our lesson can assist in eliminating some of the confusion. But first, I contend there are few misconceptions we must address.

First of all, there is a misconception that pastoral care should only be a concern for post-care (e.g., retirement plan; annuities; 401(k); IRA; or even pastor's wife's care with longstanding of service, whose husband precedes her in death).

But now, according to biblical teachings, pastoral care apparently has to do more with financially supporting a pastor/teacher *while* he labors. "Let the elders who rule well be considered worthy of double honor, especially those who work hard at preaching and teaching. For the scripture says, you shall not muzzle the ox while he is threshing and the laborer is worthy of his wages" (1 Tim. 5:17–18).

Secondly, there is a misconception that a pastor works *for* the church. As a result, we sometimes hear accusations such as, "We pay his salary!" The fact of the matter is, a pastor works for God (cf. Jer. 3:15; Acts 20:28; Eph. 4:11). The church is his residential assignment.

However, his itinerant preaching is global. Here is the point: if God called the preacher to labor and commissioned him for labor, surely He would not leave him confused as to how he is to be compensated *while* he labors.

The third misconception is actually a myth. Some suggest that a pastor ought to live a modest life and not desire much. I combat this misconception by pointing out that the Bible commands those who are rich not to be haughty and not to trust in uncertain riches but to instead trust in the living God. However, the Bible also says we are richly given all things to enjoy (1 Tim. 6:17).

What Is the Application?

There are many scriptures that govern the pastor's responsibility regarding his care for the church. But what is often overlooked is the responsibility of the church regarding its care for the pastor. The Bible is not silent when it comes to a church's responsibility in financially supporting its pastor. I believe the clearest passage in the New Testament is 1 Cor. 9:1–14. It is in this section of Paul's letter to the church at Corinth that he uses his own freedom as an illustration in defense of his use of liberty.

However, liberty is only applicable as a result of freedom established in a man's rights; and that is what Paul does in these first fourteen verses of this chapter. He deals with the rights of the preacher/pastor and the responsibility of the people whom he ministers to.

The Pastor's Basic Needs: Verses 4–6

A pastor has the right and the church the responsibility to care for a pastor's basic needs (v. 4–6). In the business world or the workplace, this is called a benefit plan. In the world of Christian ethics, I prefer to call it "The Pastor's Maintenance Plan." (See Appendix C for Pastor's Maintenance Sample.)

Note: Again, the corporate body (local church) has the responsibility of maintaining the needs and benefits for its full-time minister/ pastor.

The provisions for God's full-time worker ought to be equal or even greater than the world's full-time worker.

The Pastor's Basic Weekly Wages: Verses 7–14

According to these verses and other passages, the pastor's wages or weekly compensation should be allocated through individual pastoral support giving/love offering (cf. Num. 18:20–24; 31; 1 Sam. 9:5–10; 1 Cor. 9:11; 13; Gal. 6:6).

The key verses are 1 Corinthians 9:11, 13.

Verse 11 asks, if we have sown spiritual things for you, is it a great thing if we reap your material things? Verse 13 asks, do you not know that those who minister the holy things eat of the things of the temple, and those who serve at the altar partake of the offerings of the altar? The keyword is "partake," rendered from the Greek word *summerizomai*, which according to the Enhanced Strong's Lexicon, translates as "be partaker with; to divide at the same time, divide together; to assign a portion; to divide together with one (so that a part comes to me, a part to him).[7] The idea is that the spiritual leader of today's church continues to share a portion of the sacrificial gifts (tithes and offering) offered unto the Lord.

According to 1 Cor. 9:14, the Lord commanded (set in place; ordained [i.e., specially instituted] this designed plan for financially supporting His preacher/pastor. But now, according to 1 Cor. 9:12, a pastor can exercise his liberty of choice. He can choose not to use his rights, i.e., the people individually giving him pastoral support/love offering as a means of compensation.

What Is the Application?

Getting back to teaching the biblical basis for compensating a pastor of a church can help eradicate the conflict that centers on the issues of a pastor's salary and maintenance, which is a major crisis in most African American churches. A pastoral support giving/love offering system is a designed, ordained plan for compensating the Lord's pastor/teacher. Therefore, if it is the Lord's plan, then it has the Lord's protection.

---

7 Strong, James: *The Exhaustive Concordance of the Bible: Showing Every Word of the Text of the Common English Version of the Canonical Books, and Every Occurrence of Each Word in Regular Order*, electronic ed. Ontario : Woodside Bible Fellowship, 1996, S. G4829.

Consider also that if the Lord has ordained it, then the pastor and the people ought not to be afraid to practice it.

The Believer's Blessings
1. 2 Chronicles 31:4–10
2. Malachi 3:10–12
3. Philippians 4:15–19

In closing, notice how the Apostle Paul reminded the saints in Thessalonica to take care of their spiritual leaders.

And we urge you, brethren, to recognize those who labor among you, and are over you in the Lord and admonish you, and *esteem* them very highly in love for their work's sake. Be at peace among yourselves (1 Thess. 5:12–13).

God's people, when given the facts, will normally do the right thing.

Chapter 8

Summary and Conclusions

The primary aim of this book has focused upon the ongoing crisis regarding the holistic approach to stewardship within the African American church community and how it may be resolved. The continuing crisis in the average black church reveals a disproportionate number of weak stewards in the church's overall membership in the areas of discipleship, fellowship, serving, and giving. Therefore, many churches are not functioning properly and are failing to produce mature believers who are practicing good, balanced stewardship that is necessary for the edification of the local church as well as the church universal. Numerous churches and pastors are suffering financially; large numbers of churches are ineffectual and impotent in their service and their witness as a result of poor stewardship.

I have attempted to identify and address what I believe are the most significant ills plaguing African American churches. First and foremost, churches find themselves in crisis because there is improper organization and structure in terms of who is the governing authority in the local body. Additionally, many congregants possess a negative paradigm regarding the issue of stewardship because their views have been limited to stewardship within the context of finances rather than a holistic understanding that stewardship encompasses every aspect of a believer's life. Finally, based upon my extensive travels conducting stewardship workshops across this nation, it is clear that solid expository preaching and exegetical teaching in the area of holistic stewardship is lacking. Monetary stewardship has been taught to some degree, but many pastors and congregants have not been the recipients of a systemic teaching approach to holistic stewardship based upon timeless biblical principles.

I firmly believe that the stewardship crisis prevalent in the average African American church can be averted and possibly even eradicated if churches will adhere to what is necessary based on the precepts of the Bible. The ministry of every church leader must be clarified and taught based on the tenets found in the Word of God. Again, church structure must be properly established, and every office must function according to the scriptural mandate. Those offices, policies, and procedures (which untold numbers of churches have adopted) that are not scriptural have their place and their function but they are never to supersede God's Word. Pastors must commit themselves to equipping their lay leaders to lead, thereby demonstrating the team concept of shared ministry. Lay leaders must work hand in hand with their pastor/teacher so that the membership will utilize their spiritual gifts in becoming disciples who are thoroughly equipped for the work of ministry.

Consequently, African American churches that represent the norm can be freed from the crippling effects of the present crisis and become faithful to the divine mandate in this world, but the concept of holistic stewardship must be properly taught, clearly understood, and diligently practiced. The people of God must have a hunger and a thirst for biblical knowledge and a sincere desire to become obedient to the will of the Father as He has declared plainly in His Word. Most assuredly, the blessings tied to good stewardship are innumerable in the present and throughout eternity for those believers who seek to glorify God through their faith and obedience.

Also, financially struggling churches and pastors can cease to exist, and good stewardship in the areas of giving and pastoral support can become a reality when God's people are taught based upon His unchanging truths.

Some are asking for a new paradigm; however, rather than a new paradigm, the church must recapture the paradigm in place. Getting back to teaching basic holistic stewardship principles is the key to correcting the stewardship crisis in African American churches. As pointed out in both the Old and New Testaments, the Bible is replete with timeless holistic stewardship principles. Therefore, the African American church must reexamine its Christian education curriculum. All teaching by the church must have a focal point in mind of some facet of holistic stewardship. Recommendations may include a one-year planning calendar, weekly stewardship classes, a stewardship sermon of the month, seminars, steward-ship revivals, as well as personal stewardship training. The clergy and church must teach stewards to become stewardship trainers. Stewardship training must begin with the new member, must be embedded in the earliest years of children, and must be the mindset of the total church.

Finally, the teaching of holistic stewardship must not be allowed to appear as a simple add-on to the ministry of the church. Why? If so be it, then the stewardship crises that affect African American pastors and their congregations will continue to perpetuate, and the stewardship syndrome will continue to exist.

Glossary of Major Terms

Understanding the historical/cultural context as well as the gram-matical and syntactical structure of a text is critical to the development of a holistic approach for correcting the stewardship crisis affecting many African American churches. Defining and understanding the meaning of keywords is indispensable as we begin the first step in the process of addressing the stewardship crisis.

Holistic

According to *Merriam–Webster's Dictionary* the word "holistic" is defined as relating to or concerned with whole or with complete systems rather than with the analysis of, treatment of, or dissection into parts.[1] *Roget's 21st Century Thesaurus in Dictionary Form Third Edition* lists a variety of meanings, such as complete, whole, aggregate, com-prehensive, entire, full, integrated, total, and universal.[2]

Stewardship

In the New Testament, stewardship from the Greek word *oiko-nomia* translates as the management of a household or household affairs. It refers specifically to the management, oversight, and admin-istration of another's property.[3] In biblical times, stewardship was

---

1   *Merriam-Webster Dictionary*, s.v. "holistic."
2   *Roget's 21st Century Thesaurus in Dictionary Form*, 3rd Edition s.v. "holistic"
3   Strong, J. (1996). *The Exhaustive Concordance of the Bible* (electronic ed.):

the sense of managing and providing for a household—managing a household, running a household, or being in charge of a household.[4]

Steward

At its simplest, a "steward" is defined as a manager or overseer over another's property or possessions. It is rendered from the Greek word *oikonomos*. It is a compound word derived from *oikos,* "house," and *nemo,* "to arrange." The word originally referred to the manager of a household or estate, and then in a broader sense denoted an administrator or a steward in general.

Tithe

It is the religious act of giving one-tenth of your earnings for the support of a religious purpose."[5] A tenth of agricultural or other produce, personal income, or profits, contributed either voluntarily or as a tax for the support of the church or clergy or for charitable purposes.

Offerings

Offering is rendered from the Greek word *prosphora,* meaning that which is offered, a gift, a tribute, a present; the act of offering or a bringing to; an unused root meaning to apportion or bestow an offering to God. In this book, the word "offerings" refers to giving something over and above a tithe.

Pastor's Support/Love Offering

The Greek word *misthos,* from which the word *wages* is derived according to Louw and Nida in *Greek-English Lexicon of the New Testa-*

(G3622). Ontario: Woodside Bible Fellowship.

4   Louw, J. P., and Nida, E. A. (1996, c1989). *Greek-English Lexicon of the New Testament: Based on Semantic Domains* (electronic ed. of the 2nd edition) (Vol. 1, Page 519). New York: United Bible Societies.

5   Freedman, David Noel: *The Anchor Bible Dictionary.* New York: Doubleday, 1996, c1992, S. 6:578168 *Libronix Digital Library System on CD-Rom.*

ment: Based on Semantic Domains, may be rendered as "money on which to live" or "money for food and lodging."[6]

In this book, the terms "love offering" and "pastoral support" will be used interchangeably with wages (1 Cor. 9:1–14; 2 Cor. 11:8; Gal. 6:6–8).

Partaker

In this book, the word "partake" refers to the word Paul used in 1 Corinthians 9:13. It is a translation from the Greek word *summeri-zomai.*[7] It is derived from the Geek words *sún,* a primary preposition which denotes the idea of union or togetherness, and *merízō,* which translates to divide. Together, they form the word *summerizomai* which translates to share jointly with at the same time, or to divide into portions. [8]

Ministry

The word ministry, as used in this book, renders from the Greek word *leitourgia,* which translates to a role or assignment in service. The meaning of ministry may be expressed in some languages as a way of serving.[9]

6   Louw, Johannes P.; Nida, Eugene Albert: *Greek-English Lexicon of the New Testament : Based on Semantic Domains,* electronic ed. of the 2nd edition. New York : United Bible societies, 1996, c1989, S. 1:570.

7   Strong, James: *The Exhaustive Concordance of the Bible: Showing Every Word of the Test of the Common English Version of the Canonical Books, and Every Occurrence of Each Word in Regular Order.* Electronic ed. Ontario: Woodside Bible Fellowship. 1996, S, G4829 *Libronix Digital Library System on CD-Rom.*

8   Zodhiates, S. (2000, c1992, c1993). *The complete word study dictionary: New Testament* (electronic ed.) (G4829). Chattanooga, TN: AMG Publishers.

9   Louw, Johannes P.; Nida, Eugene Albert: *Greek-English Lexicon of the New Testament: Based on Semantic Domains.* electronic ed. of the 2nd edition. New York: United Bible Societies, 1996, c1989, S. 1:460.

Appendix A

Clarifying the Trustee's Ministry (A Sample of Qualifications and a Job Description)

The New Pilgrim Rest Baptist Church
Trustee Manual
Dr. Billy Bell, Sr. Pastor

TITLE: TRUSTEE

Definition:

The term is used for the group of people selected by the senior pastor to care for the property of the church. Some churches prefer the term "stewards." If a church is incorporated (a highly desirable procedure for state requirements only), the title of trustee may be designated in the charter. As stewards, they hold in trust for the church membership the material possessions that have been accrued by the church. An autonomous church, such as a Baptist church, holds full title to all property that is donated to it or purchased by it. The church has the inalienable right to exercise their vote on the disposition of its assets, but to comply with the laws and to be assured of skilled administration of assets, it is necessary to empower representatives to hold property, to administer it, and to handle all legal and financial details concerning it. New Pilgrim Rest Missionary Baptist Church has come to realize that it is not wise to expect the trustees, finance committee, or regular officials to prepare the annual budget. One reason is that these officials, by nature of their work, find it necessary to limit expenses as much as possible and compare the current year with the previous years for items, costs, upkeep, bills, etc.

A budget committee made up of people concerned more with the program and outreach ministries potentials, this committee will exercise less inhibited vision and faith and come up with a "dream budget" to challenge the members.

Typical Duties:

Ensure the overall maintenance and upkeep of church property in trust. Signatures of trustee are required on all deeds, transfer of stocks, bonds, IRAs, bank notes, and mortgages. The property of trustees is not assessable or involved in any failure of the church to make good on a note or other obligation. If the church is named as beneficiary in a will, the proceedings for receiving the inheritance will be arranged by the trustees. Unless the will stipulates the exact use of the bequest, the trustees will advise the church concerning the use to which it may be put to advantage.

> » Function as the channel of communication between the pastor, deacons, and the budget committee for all property improvements and the security of property.
>
> » Receive, reproduce, and distribute all copies of reports for maintaining property or improvements to deacon staff and budget committee.
>
> » Attend monthly Business meetings with deacons, finance count team, and budget committee personnel.
>
> » Prepare trustee budget request for fiscal year for property improvement, general maintenance, or land purchase.
>
> » Schedule periodical external and internal property walk-through with deacons and budget committee members to ensure all responsibilities intermesh to the extent that no individual or committee can work effectively independent of the others.
>
> » Plan and implement churchwide external and internal spring cleanup among the membership.
>
> » Assist budget staff by ensuring that all forms, requisitions, and projects requiring funding are completed and submitted in a timely manner.

»   Be responsible for implementing review process for all goals and objectives issued by the senior pastor.

»   Schedule and arrange meetings and appointments with potential contractors for budget-approved projects.

»   Handle vouchers, credit cards, and checks for the purpose of acquiring material or remuneration's purposes.

»   Supervise and assist where necessary with the completion of all Goal & Objective, and Action Step Sheets concerning property improvement.

»   Responsible for need assessment concerning the buying and selling of property.

»   Responsible for making evaluation or termination request of any employee causing property damage or inflating the budget due to negligence in his or her job performance.

»   Keep pastor informed of all matters related to building deterioration or potential advantages of purchasing property.

»   Trustees should see to it that the church carries the maximum allowable insurance on its properties. Sympathetic agencies must be found or cultivated to provide protection for these properties.

»   Review insurance company's policy for pastor hospitalization insurance and retirement to ensure that New Pilgrim Rest has provided the best policy available. After the review is complete, findings of financial obligations should be passed on to budget committed and deacons staff for implementation purposes.

»   Study all property blueprints for the purpose of being abreast of all possible expansions.

»   Ensure that all deeds, titles, and other important papers are placed in a safe deposit box or fireproof vault.

»   Be responsible for keeping down expenses as much as possible as the budget dictates for property improvement, etc.

»   Responsible for financial records auditing not less than once a year by either an able auditing committee within the church or by a certified public accounting firm.

»   Supervise all reimbursements pertaining to property improvement or purchased items that must be accompanied by a written request and receipts of item(s) purchased.

Qualifications

The character and the devotion of a trustee should be equal to that of a deacon, for the trustee is in charge of that which has been bought or given by dedicated people; much of the property represents the result of church offerings and special fund. A trustee should be practical, thrifty (not stingy), financially capable, and possess good judgment. A good credit rating (not flawless) is needed to enable trustee to sign on property purchase or loan business matters. Each trustee must fill out credit application to be placed on record. All credit reports will remain confidential and in the possession of the chairperson or co-chairperson of trustees. Trustee may request which official will retain credit report. No other committee in the church is to have access to this report. A working knowledge of law is of great benefit. A gem of a candidate is someone who is demonstrating these qualities in a business or profession, and certainly in the money matters at home.

Education

A trustee must be a high school graduate, or the equivalent, including advanced courses in business, computers, and office management practices.

Time Commitments

   A. Regular attendance at worship services (i.e., Women Ministry, Brotherhood, Sunday Morning Worship @10:30 and Sunday school.
   B. Attend at least one leadership conference a year (W.H.W. Ministries).
   C. Attend "making it happen" staff meetings as scheduled.
   D. Meet with deacon staff and budget staff once a month.
   E. Attend nine-week training course on "stewards" of God's property as outlined by the pastor.

Skills Necessary
A. Effective communication skills.
B. The ability to work well with and relate to people.
C. Organizational skills.
D. Some college or job-related experience.

Prerequisites
A. New Pilgrim Rest Membership
B. Must consistently tithe
C. Must attend Sunday school
D. Must attend Bible study and prayer service
E. Must be an active follower of pastor in outside fellowships

Selection
Senior Pastors carefully and prayerfully approve all Trustees

Appendix B

Lessons: Suggestive Tools for New Membership Training

Sample Handbook for New Members (Excerpts)

NEW MEMBERS ORIENTATION HANDBOOK

Welcome New Members

Go ye therefore, and teach all nations, baptizing them in the name of the Father, and of the Son, and of the Holy Ghost: Teaching them to observe all things whatsoever I have commanded you: and lo, I am with you always, even unto the end of the world (Matt. 28:19–20).

Our Motto:
"The church where we worship God in the beauty of holiness and magnify Jesus through the power of the Holy Spirit."

New Members Orientation

Preface

This new members' orientation handbook was designed specifically for those who profess their faith in Christ and are prepared to take on the rights and responsibilities of membership.

In compiling this book, it is our desire that it will prove to be helpful to many, regardless of age and experience, as they begin their period of growth as a babe in Christ or as they become a new member in a new family. This book explains how a new Christian functions as a member in the body of Christ and as a new member in the family of God (Eph. 5:30).

This book contains seven sessions of Christian Basic Training. Each member is required to take each session. These classes are taught each Sunday morning at 8:15 during the Sunday school hour and also each Monday night at 7:00. You are not to connect yourself with any auxiliary in the church prior to the completion of your seven sessions. Evaluation and certification is instructed and conducted by the pastor.

On behalf of the pastor and church family, we welcome you and thank you for choosing this church as your church home. We pray that it will be a blessing to you.

Welcome!
New Members Ministry

CONTENTS

~ CHURCH COVENANT ~
(Read before first and sixth session)

SESSION IA

SESSION IB

SESSION II

SESSION III

SESSION IV

SESSION V

SESSION VI

SESSION VII

New Member's Structural Flow Chart
(A Suggested Example)

ORIENTATION: New Members (Candidates for Baptism)
(Twenty-six-Week Study Curriculum)
(Six-Week Class)

New Members' Orientation Class

NM–LEV I   SURVIVAL KIT FOR NEW CHRISTIANS
(Thirteen weeks spent in this book)

1–3	The Honeymoon Stage: One Body
4–5	The Fight Stage: Two Natures
6–7	The Doubting Stage: Three Aspects of Salvation
8–9	The Panic Search for Truth Stage: Four Sources of Authority
10–13	The Silent Character Stage: The Five & Five Principle (pastor and wife will teach this class)

NM-LEV 2   LESSON ON ASSURANCE
(Five weeks spent in this class)

1	Assurance of Salvation
2	Assurance of Answered Prayer
3	Assurance of Victory
4	Assurance of Forgiveness
5	Assurance of Guidance

NM-LEV 3   LESSONS ON CHRISTIAN LIVING
(Four weeks spent in this class)

1	Putting God First
2	God's Strength
3	God's Word
4	Witnessing

NM-LEV 4   JOE T. OLDE HANDBOOK
(Four weeks spent in this class)

1	The Meaning of Church Membership
2	Christian Growth
3–4	God's Plan for Church Finance (pastor and wife will teach this class)

The New Members' Curriculum is designed for the undergirding of all new members of the church with the basic foundation of Christianity. We believe without the proper root, there will be very little fruit.

> If you abide in Me, and My words abide in you, you will ask what you desire, and it shall be done for you. By this my Father is glorified, that you bear much fruit, so you will be My disciples. John 15:7–8

Sample New Membership Stewardship Lesson
Supporting Your Pastor Spiritually and Financially

Too many of our churches are divisive in spirit and fragmented in structure as a result of ignorance to God's plan for his church. Every church's desire should be, "We want to please God." God works in the world through his church. Therefore, every member in the body of Christ must accept God's structure and plan for His church. It begins with accepting and supporting God's pastor—His gift to the local church.

Notice: The Bible instructs the people of God how to support the pastor of a church. It is twofold: spiritually and financially. However, before you can successfully do either, several considerations must be taken into account:

I. **HIS WORTH: Ephesians 4:8, 11**

   A. As members of the local church, you will never successfully support your pastor spiritually and financially until you acknowledge that his authority is divinely given (Eph. 4:11).

Notice: These scriptures suggest that God calls and chooses men to shepherd his chosen or elected.

   1. Exodus 3:1–4; 11–17: Moses' authority from God
   2. Joshua 1:1–9: Joshua's authority from God
   3. Jeremiah 1:4–10; 3:15: Authority God ordained
   4. Acts 20:28: Elders (pastors)
   5. Ephesians 4:11
      a. Apostles; Prophets: Foundational gifts (cf. Eph. 2:19–20; Eph. 4:11)
      b. Evangelists (pastor/teacher): Functional gifts into today's church (Eph. 4:11)

   B. He is the earthly head in the local church. We are to acknowledge his authority through obedience and submission.

Write out Hebrews 13:17

_____

_____

_____

_____

C. When we do an exegetical study of John 10:1–10; 14–18, here is what we discover:
1. The Master's sheep are the same sheep assigned to the pastor.
2. The sheep who hear the voice of the Master will not find it difficult to follow their pastor.
3. The Master's sheep and the pastor's sheep are the same sheep.

II. HIS WORK: Ephesians 4:12–16
A. To equip the saints to do the work of the ministry   v.12
B. Grow the saints to maturity   v.13
C. Faith builder through teaching   v.14
D. Accurately divide the word of truth   v.15
E. Encourage unanimity in the body of Christ   v.16

III. HIS WAGES
Notice: You may ask, "How can understanding the pastor's wages be significant in supporting the pastor both spiritually and financially?"
A. Just as his worth is ordained in his calling, so is his work ordained in his commission. Likewise, his wages are also ordained in compensation. The word ordained, used here, means the calling, the commission, and the method of compensation was set in place, as it was conceived in the eternal mind of God in eternity past (1 Corinthians 9:14).

Notice:
1. It is customary that who you work for pays your wages. The pastor of a church is employed by God (Jeremiah 1:5, 10; 3:15; Eph. 4:11; Acts 20:28).

2. The pastor's worth, work, and wages are tied inextricably together. His calling makes him worthy because he is a gift from God. But then his work is to "perfect the saints to do the work of the ministry." This makes his work special because he works for God. Surely God, who called him and commissioned him, would not leave him confused concerning his compensation.

B. The principle the church is to use is the only biblical principle God has ordained. Supporting a pastor financially is a spiritual matter, not a secular matter (1 Corinthians 9:11; 13–14).

1. It is done through tithes and offerings.
2. Tithes and offerings are the sacrificial gifts we continue to offer God (Mal. 3:10, 1 Corinthians 9:13–14; 16:1–2).

Note: In 1 Cor. 9:13, Paul refers back to when God first established a *purpose* for continuing the tithing principle (cf. Num. 18:20–24; 31 with 1 Cor. 9:13, 14). Here's the point:

a. According to the Old Testament, all the tithes of Israel went toward the physical support for the Levites and the priest.

b. According to the New Testament, Paul teaches that a shared portion of the tithes and a portion of the offering are used as a means to financially support today's spiritual leader. The keyword is "partaker," used in 1 Cor. 9:13. It's derived from the Greek word *summerizomai* which translates "to share jointly with; sharing a part from the whole." This introduces the pastor's support/love offering system gathered through the tithes and offerings. The New Testament teaches this principle and none other.

c. Tithing and giving offering is to be done individually by God's people (cf. Gal. 6:6) as it was ordained by the Lord (1 Cor. 9:14).

C. There are blessings for those who support God's pastors spiritually and financially.

1. Paul taught the Galatians' church the same principle as he taught other churches (Gal. 6:6).

2. The Philippians' saints were taught that God rewards those who support the man of God (Phil. 4:10–20).
    »   There will be fruit in heaven's account.   v.17
    »   When you please God, He rewards you.   v.18
    »   Support the Pastor, and God promises to supply your need.   v.19

3. When you share financially with your spiritual leader (your pastor), know that God's promises will meet your need. What a promise! (Phil. 4:19)

Appendix C

Pastor's Maintenance and Benefit Plan—Sample

	Current Year	Next Year
I. Minister's maintenance & related expenses		
A. Housing		
1. Housing rental value		
Parsonage allowance		
Utilities allowance		
2. Housing allowance		
Mortgage allowance		
Utilities allowance		
B. Transportation		
1. Auto: Includes gas, maintenance		
Insurance (Future to include Purchase or lease option)		
C. Convention expenses (workshop)		
D. Continuing education		
E. Books, periodicals, resources		
F. Expense account		
G. Vacations		
H. Miscellaneous		
II. Benefits		
A. Insurance, life insurance		
B. Retirement		
1. 401K or 403B		

	Current Year	Next Year
2. Annuities	_____	_____
C. Medical/dental plan	_____	_____
1. Family plan	_____	_____
Grand total of maintenance and related ministry expenses/benefits	_____	_____

Bibliography

Alexander, Patricia, ed. *The Family Encyclopedia of the Bible*. Chancellor Press: 1978.

Amerson, Melvin. *Stewardship in African-American Churches: A New Paradigm*. Nashville: Discipleship Resources, 2006.

Atchison, Samuel. *Christian Stewardship*. Oakland Post. Vol. 30, 1993.

Barna, George, and Harry R. Jackson Jr. *High Impact African-American Churches*. Ventura: Regal Books from Gospel Light, 2004.

Berquist, Millard J. *Studies in First Corinthians*. Nashville: Convention Press, 1960.

Brazell, George. *Dynamic Stewardship Strategies: Harnessing Time, Talent, and Treasury for Church Growth*. Grand Rapids: Baker Book House, 1989.

Boice, James Montgomery. *Foundations of the Christian Faith*. Downers Grove, Illinois: InterVarsity Press, 1986.

Bruce, F. F. *The Book of the Acts*. Grand Rapids: Wm. B. Erdmans Publishing Co., 1988.

Bruce, Guy. *Bastian Union Church History*, journal online, accessed 13 June 2006, available from http://www.bland.k12.va.us/bland/Rocky/bastianunion.html.

Burkett, Larry. *Giving and Tithing: Includes Serving and Stewardship*. Chicago: Moody Press, 1991.

Calvin, John. *Institutes of the Christian Religion*. Philadelphia: Westminster Press, 1960.

Cully, Iris V. and Kendig Brubaker Cully, ed. *Harper's Encyclopedia of Religious Education*. San Francisco: Harper & Row Publishers, Inc., 1990.

Drane, John, ed. *The New Lion Encyclopedia of the Bible*. Lion Publishing: 1998.

Easton, M. G. *Easton's Bible Dictionary*. Oak Harbor: Logos Research Systems, Inc., 1996.

Eichrodt, Walther. *Theology of the Old Testament*. SCM Press, 1961.

Frazier, Franklin. *The Negro Church in America*. New York: Schocken Books, 1974.

Gaebelein, Frank E. *The Expositor's Bible Commentary.* Grand Rapids: The Zondervan Corporation, 1976.

Gill, Ben. *Stewardship: The Biblical Basis for Living.* Arlington: The Summit Publishing Group, 1996.

Heerspink, Robert. *Becoming a Firstfruits Congregation.* Grand Rapids: CRC Publications, 1996.

Jenkins, Lee. *Taking Care of Business: Establishing a Financial Legacy for the African American Family.* Chicago: Moody Press, 2001.

Jones, Clifford A. Sr. *From Proclamation to Practice.* Valley Forge: Judson Press, 1993.

Jones, Major J. *Black Awareness: A Theology of Hope.* Nashville: Abingdon Press, 1971.

Lincoln, C. Eric, and Lawrence H. Mamiya. *The Black Church in the African-American Experience.* Durham: Duke University Press, 1990.

MacArthur, John. *Giving God's Way.* Wheaton: Tyndale House Publishers, Inc., 1986.

MacArthur, John. *God's Plan for Giving.* Chicago: Moody Press, 1982.

MacArthur, John. *The MacArthur Study Bible.* Word Publishing, a division of Thomas, Nelson, Inc., 1997.

Martin, Alfred. *Biblical Stewardship.* Iowa: ECS Ministries, 2005.

Merriam–Webster's Collegiate Dictionary, Tenth Edition.

Mukenge, Ida Rousseau. *The Black Church in Urban America: A Case Study in Political Economy.* Lanham: University Press of America, Inc., 1941.

Montgomery, John. *Money, Power, Greed: Has the Church Been Sold Out?* Ventura: Regal Books, 1987.

Orr, J., MA, DD. *The International Standard Bible Encyclopedia: 1915 edition* (J. Orr, Ed.). Albany, OR: Ages Software, 1999.

Pinn, Anne H. and Anthony B. Pinn, *Fortress Introduction to Black Church History*, Minneapolis: Fortress Press, 2002.

Raboteau, Albert J. *Canaan Land: A Religious History of African Americans.* New York: Oxford University Press, 1999.

Radmacher, Earl D., Ronald Barclay Allen, and H. Wayne House. *Nelson's New Illustrated Bible Commentary.* Nashville: T. Nelson Publishers, 1999.

Rodin, R. Scott. *Stewards in the Kingdom: A Theology of Life in All Its Fullness.* Downers Grove, Illinois: InterVarsity Press, 2000.

Roget's 21st Century Thesaurus in Dictionary Form, 3rd Edition.

Rolston, Holmes. *Stewardship in the New Testament Church.* Richmond: John Know Press, 1946.

Steward, Austin and Benjamin Paul, *Austin Steward 1794–1860* [journal online] accessed 13 June 2006.

Smith, T. Dewitt Jr. *New Testament Deacon Ministry in African-American Churches*. Atlanta: Hope Publishing House, 1994.

Strong, James. *The Exhaustive Concordance of the Bible: Showing Every Word of the Test of the Common English Version of the Canonical Books, and Every Occurrence of Each Word in Regular Order*. Electronic ed. Ontario: Woodside Bible Fellowship, 1996. *Libronix Digital Library System on CD-Rom*.

Swenson, Richard A., MD. *The Overload Syndrome: Learning to Live Within Your Limits*. Colorado Springs: NavPress, 1999.

Tsevat, Matitiahu. *The Basic Meaning of the Biblical Sabbath*. Zettschrift fur die Alttestamin Hiche Wissenschraft, 1972.

Vallet, Ronald E. *Congregations at the Crossroads: Remembering to Be Households of God*. Grand Rapids: William B. Eerdmans Publishing Company, 1998.

Vallet, Ronald E. *Stepping Stones of the Steward: A Faith Journey through Jesus' Parables*. Grand Rapids: William B. Eerdmans Publishing Company, 1994.

Vallet, Ronald E. *The Steward Living in Covenant*. Grand Rapids: William B. Eerdmans Publishing Company, 2001.

Wilkinson, Loren. *Earthkeeping: Christian Stewardship of Natural Resources*. William B. Erdmans Publishing Company, 1980.

Williams, Juan, and Quinton Dixie. *This Far by Faith*. New York: Harper Collins Publishers, 2003.

Witherington, Ben III. *The Acts of the Apostles: A Socio-Rhetorical Commentary*. Grand Rapids: William B. Eerdmans Publishing Co., 1998.

Youngblood, R. F., Bruce, F. F., Harrison, R. K. *Nelson's New Illustrated Bible Dictionary*. Thomas Nelson Publishers, 1995.

About the Author

Dr. George W. Banks Jr, formerly a native of Monroe, Louisiana, founder and president of Faith Works Stewardship Ministries, is an author, workshop facilitator, conference speaker, and former senior pastor of the Graceland Community Baptist Church in Santa Ana, California. With twenty-seven years of pastoral experience, Dr. Banks has spent many years teaching, training, and leading Christians and churches back to spiritual truths.

Widely known for his work in resolving stewardship issues, Dr. Banks maintains a brisk speaking schedule. He travels extensively, ministering to churches throughout this nation and abroad, conducting workshops and conferences, and sharing biblical principles of Christian stewardship for a believing people.

He boldly proclaims, "When godly principles are practiced, godly promises will prevail." He is also known for his many infamous statements such as,

> One cannot rightfully worship God in principle and be a bad steward in practice; worship, leadership, fellowship, and discipleship—all these "ships"—are rooted in stewardship.

> You will never get out of debt with man, staying in debt with God.

and his most often quoted statement in many churches today,

> God's people, given the facts, will normally do the right thing.

Currently, Dr. Banks is a member of the pastoral family at the Fellowship Baptist Church of Oak Cliff in Dallas, Texas, where he serves as pastor of stewardship studies. He is also stewardship specialist for the National Evangelism Training Workshop of America, headquartered in Oakland, California.

Dr. Banks earned his BA in psychology from California State University, Los Angeles, California. He also earned his MDiv and DMin degrees from Faith Evangelical Seminary, Tacoma, Washington. He and his wife, Claudia, reside in Denton, Texas.

To host a stewardship workshop or conference, please contact:

Dr. George W. Banks
Faith Works Stewardship Ministries
PO Box 51099
Denton, Texas 76206
Phone: 940-382-8379 · 714-654-2803
Fax: 940-382-8279

Printed in the United States
100562LV00005B/286-399/A

9 781587 369100